BLUE GUIDE

PILGRIM'S ROME

A BLUE GUIDE TRAVEL MONOGRAPH

A.B. Barber

Somerset Books • London

CONTENTS

Angel on Ponte Sant'Angelo holding the veil of Veronica. Known as the vernicle, the veil with the imprint of Christ's face became to Rome what the scallop shell was to Compostela, the badge worn by pilgrims who had made the journey.

PILGRIM'S ROME

'Go thou to Rome,—at once the Paradise, the grave, the city and the wilderness...'

The words are those of Percy Bysshe Shelley, Romantic poet and atheist, from his *Adonaïs*, an elegy on the death of John Keats, who died in Rome in 1821 and is buried in the Protestant Cemetery beside the old city walls.

Perhaps it seems strange, in the first chapter of a book about pilgrimage, to be quoting the work of an atheist. But Rome is no respecter of persons: the city exerts its magnetic pull on everyone. We might find ourselves kneeling in front of the altar of St Lawrence, because it contains a part of the gridiron upon which the saint was roasted for his faith in AD 258, or we might choose to stand in line outside the church of Santa Maria in Cosmedin, waiting to have our photograph taken with one hand in the jaws of the Bocca della Verità, because Gregory Peck and Audrey Hepburn did it in *Roman Holiday*. The impulse to tread where others trod before us, and to recall their deeds, is very strong.

And Rome is an easy city to get around. As the map (overleaf) shows, it lies conveniently strung out along the Tiber's north–south axis. The ancient city, sprawled across its famous seven hills, stood on the east bank, while west of the river was the district of *Transtiberim*, the modern Trastevere, home to a community of Jews and, later, to Christians. From this dense heart, the arterial consular roads radiated out: the Via Salaria and Via Nomentana to the northeast; the Via Tiburtina and Via Praenestina to the east; the Via Aurelia to the west; and in the south the Via Ostiensis, leading to the port of Ostia, the great mouth via which the belly of Rome was fed with North African corn. It was close to this road, at Tre Fontane, that St Paul was martyred, and just beside it, under San Paolo fuori le Mura, that he now lies entombed.

Those ancient roads still exist, or at least, modern roads do, that follow the ancient routes. The most famous of all the roads, still paved in sections with ancient basalt slabs, lies to the southeast: the Via Appia, site of the most celebrated catacombs. It is along the Via Appia that St Paul arrived in Rome, and along the same road that St Peter tried to flee it.

The road that leads north from the city, the Via Flaminia, preserves its straight lines within the centre as the Via del Corso, always filled with traffic and pedestrians, and with famous landmarks on either side: the Spanish Steps and Trevi Fountain to the east and the Pantheon to the west.

The modern city flings itself widely over both Tiber banks. The river lies between, deeply entrenched, fringed by plane trees and bordered by busy roads, the *lungoteveri*. It flows so far below the level of the modern

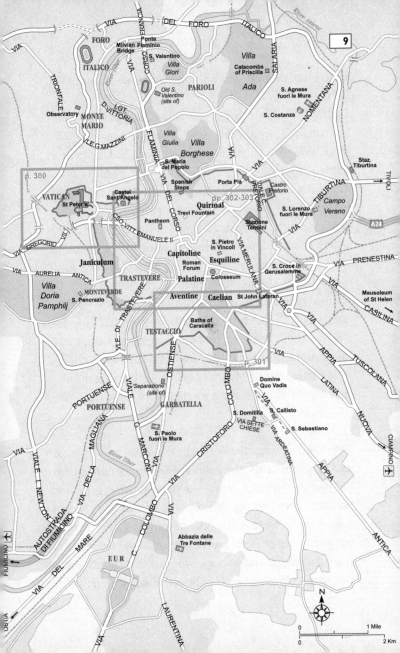

streets that its green-brown waters are invisible until you get close.

Above the Tiber to the east is the Aventine Hill, leafy and tranquil. In ancient times it had a reputation as a place of foreign cults. Christianity flourished there, as its many early churches show. On the west bank north of Trastevere are the Vatican City and St Peter's, an area that never lay within the ancient metropolis, being instead a verdant suburb of fields and gentle hills, dotted with patrician villas and traversed by roadways lined with tombs, as was the Roman custom.

The hill of Monte Mario, north of the Vatican, was the vantage point from which medieval pilgrims making their way to Rome from across the Alps would have had their first sight of the Eternal City, spread out before them like a promise of hope and salvation. They knew the hill as *Mons Gaudii*, the Mount of Rejoicing, because the view they had from its summit so gladdened their weary and expectant hearts.

The word pilgrim derives from the Latin *per* (beyond) and *agri* (the fields, the countryside). In its purest original sense it simply denotes a person coming in from without. It still means that, but the 'inside' and the 'outside' have become metaphorical terms. A pilgrimage is not so much a physical journey as a spiritual one. 'Faith is the substance of things hoped for, the evidence of things not seen.' (*Hebrews 11:1*). The men and women of the

Old Testament 'all died in faith, not having received the promises, but having seen them afar off, and embraced them, and confessed that they were strangers and pilgrims on the earth. For they that say such things declare plainly that they seek a country.' The Pilgrim Fathers who colonised America declared overtly that they were seeking a country. Pilgrims to Rome are seeking a country too, but in an emblematic, transcendental way: 'A better country, that is, an heavenly.'

'Hurry!' wrote Cecil Day Lewis in a poem entitled *Flight to Italy*,

'We burn
For Rome so near us, for the phoenix moment
When we have thrown off this traveller's trance,
And mother-naked and ageless-ancient
Wake in her warm nest of renaissance.'

This book takes you on a tour of Rome's principal Christian sites, beginning with the shrines of the apostles Peter and Paul and the famous 'seven churches' of the early pilgrim tradition, moving on through the areas of the city where early Christians lived and visiting the catacombs where they were laid to rest. Famous monuments of pagan Rome are also explored, along with their relationship to the Christian city. The pilgrim's reward for their pious journey—absolution from earthly punishment for sin— is discussed in the appendix.

AD LIMINA APOSTOLORUM
ON THE TRAIL OF ST PETER & ST PAUL

Ad limina apostolorum, literally 'to the thresholds of the apostles', is the expression used to denote a pilgrimage to the burial places of St Peter and St Paul, who suffered martyrdom under Nero around AD 64 and 65 respectively, and were both buried at Rome[1]. The following itineraries attempt to trace their footsteps through the city.

ON THE TRAIL OF ST PETER

Simon Peter, the fisherman of Lake Gennesareth, brother of St Andrew and the disciple who denied Christ, was also the first of the Twelve to see an appearance of the resurrected Saviour. He ultimately rewarded Christ's trust in him by faithfully spreading the Word as Apostle to the Jews. He features prominently in the book of Acts. We meet him urging the disciples to choose a twelfth member to replace Judas (Matthias is chosen; *Acts 1*[2]); proclaiming at Pentecost that he and the disciples are speaking in tongues not through drunkenness but through the power of the Holy Spirit (and thereby inspiring about three

---

1 Catholic bishops still make *ad limina* visits, in principle every five years.
2 His relics are claimed by the basilica of Santa Maria Maggiore (*see p. 90*).

thousand people to baptism; *Acts 2*); and healing a lame man (*Acts 3*). His fame as a healer incurs the wrath of the Sadducees and he is cast into prison, only to be freed by an angel of the Lord (*Acts 5*). We then see him raising Tabitha from the dead (*Acts 9*) and baptising Cornelius the centurion and his companions, all uncircumcised Gentiles (for, as he says, 'God is no respecter of persons', and those whom the law deems unclean may be clean in God's sight; *Acts 10*). From this time onward the disciples preach not only to Jews but to people of all nations.

Peter's second imprisonment in Jerusalem, at the time of Herod Agrippa, is recounted in Acts 12. When again freed by the angel of the Lord, we are told that he 'departed and went into another place'. We see him once more in Caesarea, then in Jerusalem, and then he disappears. Nevertheless, the tradition that his final mission took him to Rome, and that he was the first head of its Church and there suffered martyrdom, is an ancient and tenacious one. It is Peter who is credited with instituting the episcopal/papal succession: in lists of popes, Peter traditionally appears as the first. His pre-eminence among the apostles is expressed in Christ's famous words: 'Thou art Peter and upon this rock[3] I will build my church; and the gates of hell shall not prevail against it. And I will give unto thee the keys of the kingdom of heaven: and whatsoever thou shalt bind on earth shall be bound in heaven:

---

3   A pun on the name Peter, which means 'rock' in Greek.

and whatsoever thou shalt loose on earth shall be loosed in heaven.' (*Matthew 16:13–19*).

Peter's wide appeal lies partly in the fact that he was, according to Acts 4:13, 'unlearned and ignorant'. His testimony of Christ, as noted down in Greek by his proselyte and interpreter Mark in the second Gospel, concentrates on the kind of things that someone of rude understanding could readily grasp: tangible deeds such as the casting out of demons, the healing of the sick and raising of the dead. He does not dally with intellectual ideas about the Kingdom of Heaven, nor with recondite parables or philosophy.

The story of his ministry and martyrdom at Rome is based on long-embedded tradition. Two epistles of Peter survive in scripture. The first one is written from a place which he terms 'Babylon'. In the absence of any evidence or tradition linking him with the ruined Babylon on the Euphrates, commentators have interpreted the word to mean Rome, in all her wanton luxury, just as St John refers to Rome as 'Babylon' in the Book of Revelation[4].

In about the tenth year of his reign, after the great fire which burned Rome to the ground, the emperor Nero

---

4   In fact, some scholars believe that Peter came to Rome twice. Suetonius tells us that Jews were expelled from Rome by the emperor Claudius (reigned 41–54) because of tensions among them caused by conversions to Christianity (*but see p. 212*). Someone must have been here to baptise those people and to found that early community. Who if not Peter?

unleashed a terrible pogrom against the city's Christian population, St Peter among them. Peter escaped from the prison where he had been flung and was preparing to flee the city when he had a vision of Christ which caused him to turn back and face his fate. According to a tradition derived from the apocryphal Acts of Peter and supported by the third-century theologian Origen, Peter was crucified, head downwards by choice, in the Circus of Nero on the Vatican Hill and buried close by. In the apocryphal text, Peter expounds his reasons: the upside-down position mimics that of a child being born; thus it is that man is born into eternal life. He also advances the idea of needing to make the left right and the right left: to reverse our perceptions in order to understand heaven. By the time the Acts of Peter were declared apocryphal in the fifth century, much of their content had passed into the popular Roman tradition.

The place where Peter's body was laid to rest, the *Campus Petri*, became a place of pilgrimage and other Christians sought to be buried nearby. At some time in the fourth century, a basilica was erected on the site, either by Constantine or by his son Constans. Greatly enlarged and embellished, that basilica is now the largest church in the world. At its high altar, only the pope may celebrate Mass.

In art, Peter is usually depicted as an elderly, white-haired man with a square face and a bushy beard, holding a pair of keys. Peter was enjoined by Christ to 'feed my sheep' (*John 21*), an exhortation which he himself takes

up in his first epistle, urging his recipients to 'Feed the
flock of God which is among you'. The Latin and Greek
inscription around the easternmost dome of St Peter's basilica alludes to this too: 'O pastor of the Church, thou
feedest all Christ's lambs and sheep.'

We may imagine Peter here, and in all these Roman
places, as we tread in his footsteps, visiting the locations
associated with his name. Those locations are as follows:

Santa Pudenziana
Map p. 303, E2. Open 9–12 & 3–6.
Via Cavour is a busy, noisy and unlovely street, straight
and businesslike and unmeandering, driven along the
valley at the foot of the Esquiline Hill in 1890 as part
of the modernisation of the city when it finally became
the capital of united Italy, ending the temporal reign
of Pope Pius IX. It is named after Camillo Cavour, the
Piedmontese statesman who served as Italy's first Prime
Minister. On Via Urbana, a quiet street just south of this
busy thoroughfare and close to the basilica of Santa Maria
Maggiore, is a small church built upon the ruins of an
ancient bath house, which in turn was raised adjacent to
the *titulus* (*see p. 122*) of a senator named Pudens, a Christian convert said to have given hospitality to St Peter. The
church even preserves a piece of a wooden altar table at
which St Peter is alleged to have celebrated Mass.

The chief glory of Santa Pudenziana is its apse mosaic,
dating from the late fourth century. It shows Christ en-

Mosaic of Christ and the Apostles, c. 390, in the apse of Santa Pudenziana. Flanking the cross above Christ's head are the symbols of the Evangelists: man (Matthew); lion (Mark); bull (Luke); eagle (John).

throned with the disciples seated around him, Peter on the right and Paul on the left (at the bottom, the two outermost disciples have been lost, following a remodelling of the apse). Behind Peter and Paul stand two female figures holding wreaths. They symbolise the two Apostles' respective missions to the Jews and the Gentiles. Behind Christ stretches the heavenly city, with the symbols of the Evangelists floating in the sky above, flanking the hill of Calvary with its jewelled cross. Christ is clad in a rich robe and the apostles wear togas. Many scholars have pointed out the deliberate echo that this would have produced during church services, when the bishop was seated on his throne in the apse below, with his clergy on either side of him, on their semicircular synthronon. Prominent on Christ's robe is a motif that looks like a letter L. Known to scholars as a gammadion (there are many types; *see p. 175*), this L-shaped figure represents a corner-stone: 'Wherefore also it is contained in the scripture, Behold, I lay in Sion a chief corner-stone, elect, precious: and he that believeth on him shall not be confounded.' (*1 Peter 2:6.*)

The Mamertine Prison
Map p. 302, C3. Open 9–4 every day. Entrance up the steps to the side of the church of San Giuseppe dei Falegnami. Entry fee.

Yea, I think it meet, as long as I am in this tabernacle, to stir you up by putting you in remembrance; Knowing that shortly I must put off this my tabernacle, even as our Lord Jesus Christ hath shewed me.   2 Peter 1:13–14

Below the little church of San Giuseppe dei Falegnami, 'St Joseph of the Woodworkers', at the foot of the Capitoline Hill, lies the famous Mamertine Prison, in ancient times known as the Tullianum, where important political prisoners were held securely, on the fringes of the Forum, just above the Senate House. From the days of the Roman republic up until the late empire, many famous captives languished here, among them Jugurtha, King of Numidia, who starved to death within these walls in 104

Detail of the carved wooden door of the Mamertine Prison showing St Peter (left, with keys and characteristic curly hair) and Paul (right, with sword and characteristic pointed beard).

BC. Vercingetorix, leader of the Gauls, was kept here after his defeat by Julius Caesar, and was finally paraded in Caesar's triumph in the Forum before being strangled. Another victim was Simon bar Giora, leader of the Jewish uprising against Rome, who was brought to the capital when the rebellion was crushed in AD 70 and kept here until he too was paraded and then executed in the triumph of the emperor Titus (Titus' triumphal arch still stands in the Forum, with Jewish symbols carved upon it; *see p. 211*). Sejanus, head of the Praetorian Guard in the reign of Tiberius, was strangled here after his fall from favour in AD 31. Had Cleopatra not killed herself with a snakebite, she too might have found herself immured in this noisome place, with the low ceiling above her head and the perpetually damp floor beneath her proud feet.

Here too, according to tradition, St Peter was taken,   and it is also asserted that St Paul was held here prior to his martyrdom. Bold lettering on the façade announces the spot as, *Prigione dei SS Apostoli Pietro e Paolo*, 'Prison of the Most Holy Apostles Peter and Paul'. Above the inscription there is a small carving of the two saints behind bars. There is no firm evidence that either saint was incarcerated here, but neither is there evidence to the contrary—and both of them must have been imprisoned somewhere.

Visitors today are shown into an upper room, where a plaque has been placed commemorating Vercingetorix, and where, on the wall at the top of the stairs, behind iron bars, a rough depression in the rock is said to preserve the imprint of St Peter's face. A short, winding stair leads you down to the prison itself. In St Peter's day there would have been no stairway: prisoners would have been summarily bundled into the lower chamber through a hole in the floor.

The undercroft is a small, cramped, cheerless place, but furnished with an altar and fitted out as a chapel, so that one cannot quite conjure up the sufferings of those who dwelt and died here. There is a little circular well in the floor, a spring which St Peter is said to have caused to rise from the rock in order that he might baptise his gaolers. Though charming, this story is completely fanciful; the well is older than that. Nevertheless, the gaolers are important to the legend, for it is through their connivance that St Peter is said to have escaped from here.

San Pietro in Vincoli
Map p. 303, E3. Open 8–12.30 & 3–6 (7 in summer).
The beautiful church of San Pietro in Vincoli preserves part of the iron chain with which St Peter is said to have been fettered in the Mamertine Prison. It is kept below the high altar in a small, glass-fronted casket. You can view it by going down the steps into the confessio. There are kneelers there, and you can light a candle.

Originally there were two chains: one of them the chain with which Herod Agrippa had bound St Peter in Jerusalem; the other the chain with which Nero had bound him in the Mamertine Prison. In around AD 439, the first chain came into the possession of the Byzantine empress Eudocia, wife of Theodosius II, who had gone to Jerusalem to offer thanks for the marriage of her daughter Eudoxia to Valentinian III, emperor of the western empire at Rome. Eudocia sent the chain to Eudoxia, and Eudoxia in turn presented it to Pope Leo I. On comparing it to the Mamertine chain already in the papal possession, Leo was dumbfounded to see the two chains miraculously become fused, a story which is interesting chiefly for its symbolic value and also for what it might tell us about the political advantage Pope Leo could see in fostering such a legend. Eudoxia founded a church to house her

Casket in San Pietro in Vincoli containing the lengths of chain said to have bound St Peter in Jerusalem and Rome.

wondrous relic. This Basilica Eudoxiana later became known as St Peter ad Vincula: 'St Peter in Bonds'.

The casket in which the chains are kept (*illustrated above*) is decorated on the top with a figure of the angel leading Peter to his destiny. It is embossed below with the crossed keys, symbol of Peter's apostolate, and the inverted cross, symbol of his martyrdom.

Most visitors to the church come to see Michelangelo's *Moses*; which is at the end of the south aisle. There will most likely be a large crowd to your right as you view the chains. The sculpture was carved in 1515 to adorn the tomb of Pope Julius II. The tomb was never finished.

Santi Nereo e Achilleo

Map p. 301, C2. Not regularly open.

And when Herod would have brought him forth, the same night Peter was sleeping between two soldiers, bound with two chains: and the keepers before the door kept the prison. And, behold, the angel of the Lord came upon him, and a light shined in the prison: and he smote Peter on the side, and raised him up, saying, Arise up quickly. And his chains fell off from his hands. And the angel said unto him, Gird thyself, and bind on thy sandals. And so he did. And he saith unto him, Cast thy garment about thee, and follow me.   Acts 12:6–8

Thus is St Peter delivered from his second imprisonment in Jerusalem. The angel of the Lord conducts him to freedom, to perhaps twenty more years of ministry. But Peter is condemned to prison again, in Rome. And this time the angel of the Lord does not appear. It is his gaolers who release him, and Peter hastens off, towards the Appian Way, meaning to flee the city. We can almost trace the line of his flight, across the Forum, around the western flank of the Palatine Hill, past the Circus Maximus, through the Porta Capena, and out towards the Via Appia. On the present-day Via delle Terme di Caracalla, named for the great Baths of Caracalla, which in St Peter's day did not exist, stands the church of Sts Nereus and Achilleus (Nereo e Achilleo), with a very faded *trompe l'oeil* façade that once showed a pediment, volutes, marble panels and other architectural elements but which is now almost worn away. The inscription over the door names the church as the *Titulus Fasciolae*, 'Titulus of the Bandage', for it is here, so they say, that during St Peter's headlong dash from the city, one of the dressings fell from a lesion on his leg caused by his heavy chains.

The church is dedicated to Sts Nereus and Achilleus, martyred soldier brothers from the imperial army, whose relics were brought here from the Catacombs of Domitilla in the early ninth century.

On the opposite side of the wide roadway stands the church of **San Sisto Vecchio**, dedicated to the martyred pope Sixtus II. According to legend the pope met St Lawrence here, three days before he was done to death in the catacombs in the year 258. St Lawrence was a victim of the same wave of persecutions. The small monastery attached to the church was the first residence in Rome of St Dominic.

Domine Quo Vadis

Map p. 9 and beyond map p. 301, D3. Open 8–6.30. Bus 218 from outside St John Lateran (stop on corner of Via dell'Amba Aradam). Get off at the stop on the Via Appia outside the L'Incontro bar.

Verily, verily, I say unto thee, When thou wast young, thou girdedst thyself, and walkedst whither thou wouldest: but when thou shalt be old, thou shalt stretch forth thy hands, and another shall gird thee, and carry thee whither thou wouldest not.   *John 21:18*

This tiny church on a bend in the Via Appia is dedicated to the Madonna delle Piante, Our Lady of Lamentations, but it is always popularly known as Domine Quo Vadis. Legend has it that it was on this spot, as he was fleeing the city, that St Peter had a vision of Christ.

Throughout the Acts and also in his epistles, Peter makes repeated reference to witness. For him it is of compelling importance to remind people that he saw all that happened with his own eyes. For Peter, seeing is believing: 'For we have not followed cunningly devised fables when we made known unto you the power and coming of our Lord Jesus Christ, but were eyewitnesses of his majesty' (*2 Peter 1:16*). Thus it is entirely appropriate that this tactile and uncerebral man should have been sent to his own martyrdom by a visible manifestation of Jesus. As he tries to run away from Rome and from his fate, he sees Christ coming towards him along the Via Appia. 'Domine, quo vadis?', he enquires, 'My Lord, where are you going?', to which Christ replies that he is on his way to Rome, to be crucified a second time, in place of Peter. Ashamed of the impulse which had led him to try to escape the inevitable, St Peter turns back, and bravely submits himself to his destiny.

The church takes the form of a single nave, prettily furnished with wooden chairs and kneelers. At the head of

Copy of the stone which purports to preserve the footmarks left by Christ after he confronted St Peter on the Appian Way. The original stone is kept in the basilica of San Sebastiano (see p. 102).

the nave, on the left, is a wall-painting of St Peter, standing on the Roman basalt slabs of the Appian Way, with the legend '*Domine Quo Vadis*' below him. On the opposite side is Christ with his reply: '*Venio Romam, iterum crucifigi.*' Between the two paintings, set into the floor and protected by an iron grille, is a block of stone (not basalt) with two crude footprints sunk into it, a symbol of the encounter between Christ and his great disciple—though the footmarks do purport to be the genuine prints of Christ. When I last visited the church, a devout Armenian had collected stones from the road and was rubbing them on the prints to make relics by contact. Moments later a party of loud German children arrived and stood on the stone to see if their own feet would fit.

A bust of Henryk Sienkiewicz, author of the historical novel *Quo Vadis*, stands at the church's west end. St Peter appears as a major character in the novel: we see him preaching, baptising and leading commemorative feasts at the catacombs.

The Catacombs of San Sebastiano

Map p. 9 and beyond map p. 301, D3. Bus 218 from outside St John Lateran (stop on corner of Via dell'Amba Aradam), or walk from Domine Quo Vadis as described below. Open 9–12 & 2–5. Closed Sun. NB: For more on other catacombs and on catacombs in general, see p. 105.

From Domine Quo Vadis, a private road signed in yellow, *'Entrata Riservata alle Catacombe San Callisto'*, leads between the Via Appia and Via Ardeatina. It makes a very peaceful way to approach the catacombs on foot. After a short while the road turns into an avenue lined with cypresses, inhabited by green parakeets. On either side the land is given over to sheep grazing and to plantations of olive trees. On your left you pass the Catacombs of San Callisto (*see p. 111*). The road curves around the large building of the Salesian Institute and brings you out onto the Via Appia. Turn right and very soon, on your right, you come to the small basilica of San Sebastiano. The entrance to the catacombs is to the right of the church.

Visits to the catacombs are by guided tour only. You will be taken down into the labyrinth of tunnels carved in the soft tufa rock, where the burial places are a mixture of loculi (wall ledges), arcosolia (arched recesses) and family chapels.

A highlight of the tour is the Crypt of St Sebastian, a chapel where the saint's remains were kept until the

seventeenth century, when they were transferred to the
basilica above. In another area of the catacombs, a part
that was once open to the sky, three fine pagan tombs are
preserved, created in disused shafts of the stone quarry
which pre-dated the burial ground. They are house-type
mausolea, with wall-paintings of banqueting and pastoral
scenes, motifs which are not so very far removed from
those used by the early Christians.

The special interest of these catacombs, from the point
of view of St Peter, is in the area known as the Triclia.
Here the walls are covered with pottery fragments,
mounted behind perspex, scratched with the names of
Peter and Paul. There are various theories: perhaps the
bodies of the two Apostles were transferred here for temporary safekeeping in 258, during the persecutions of the
emperor Valerian. Perhaps St Peter lived in a house on
this site. Or perhaps the feasts of the two martyrs were
celebrated here, rather than at their tombs, in the years
before Christianity received official, legal sanction. Whatever the truth, it is certain that St Peter was widely venerated on this spot in early Christian times.

The tour ends in the basilica, which preserves relics of St
Sebastian, who was martyred in Rome in the third century. The basilica is described more fully on p. 101.

Santa Maria in Traspontina

Map p. 300, D2. Open 8–12 & 4–6.

The church of St Mary-beyond-the-Bridge preserves, in

its third north chapel, two stumps of red marble column, one on either side of a seventeenth-century altarpiece showing St Peter and St Paul being lashed to similar columns, with Ionic capitals, prior to being scourged. The altar itself is flanked by two further red columns with Corinthian capitals. The effect of these columns in triplicate, the stump, the flanking column and the painted column, is quite curious.

The two column relics are hesitant in their claims to authenticity. It is possible that St Peter was tied to such a column and scourged before his crucifixion. St Paul would almost certainly not have been. He was a Roman citizen, and as such was treated to a swifter method of execution. To left and right of the altar are wall-paintings of the two saints' martyrdoms.

The tomb of St Peter

The site of the Circus of Nero (also known as the Circus of Caligula), the most likely place of St Peter's martyrdom, lies along the south flank of St Peter's basilica, with its curved end roughly at the point where St Peter's Square meets Via della Conciliazione and with its straight end roughly on a line with the basilica apse (this is how it is shown on the plan overleaf, though some experts believe it was orientated the other way). To the north of the circus lay a street of tombs dating from the first to the fourth centuries, culminating in a great mass of burials clustering around what is held to be the grave of St Peter.

The sumptuous Baroque basilica that we see today is the successor to a smaller church built by order of Constantine or one of his sons over the site of that grave, the spot where the body of the martyred Apostle was laid to rest. The grave is still there, but it has had several layers built around it over the years and now lies like a Russian doll, many times encased and difficult to access.

NB: The description below deals only with the tomb of St Peter. To read about St Peter's basilica, see p. 70.

The street of tombs
Admission is by previous appointment only. Visitors must be over fifteen. Guided tours lasting approx. 90mins are given to groups of a maximum of twelve people. To book, email scavi@ fsp.va or Fax: +39 06 6987 3017. To apply in person, go to the Ufficio Scavi (left of the basilica; ask the Swiss Guard to let you through), which is open Mon–Sat 9–5. Don't expect a response for several weeks. If you do not have time to wait, you can take a superb virtual tour at www.vatican.va/various/ basiliche/necropoli/scavi_english.html.

The street of tombs is a narrow alleyway with brick-built mausolea on two sides. Most of the burials are pagan; the only purely Christian tomb is Mausoleum M, the third-century family mausoleum of the Julii. On its vault, Christ appears as *Sol Novus*, the 'New Sun', shown beardless and dressed in Roman garb, driving a chariot, with a

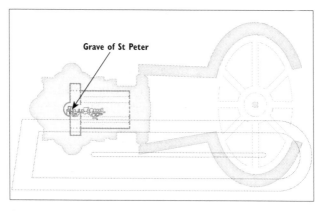

Plan of the burial site of St Peter, showing the outline of the current St Peter's Basilica and St Peter's Square with the original fourth-century basilica beneath and the street of tombs below that. The position of the Circus of Nero is indicated by a dotted line.

globe in his left hand and brilliant rays emanating from his head. The iconography is clearly derived from images of pagan sun-worship, which was instituted by the emperor Marcus Aurelius at the end of the second century. Images in the mausoleum that have no pagan derivation but which are purely Christian include Jonah and the whale and a scene of a fisherman casting his line a hooking a large fish.

In the large, mainly pagan Mausoleum H (second century), with its family busts and stuccoed niches, is a Christian inscription asking Peter to pray 'for the holy Christians buried beside your body'.

The site of Peter's grave is marked on the plan on the previous page. It takes the form of an empty space beneath a commemorative monument of the mid-second century known as the Tropaion of Gaius, which is built up against a wall plastered in red. This wall bears the name of the saint in Greek letters: ΠΕΤΡ… (the rest is missing).

Peter's original grave would have been no more than a simple mound of earth. Many other burials crowd around this space. In front of the red wall is a later wall, scratched with pilgrims' names. The bones of an elderly and well-built man were found here in 1965. They showed signs of having been disturbed, which might support the theory that St Peter's remains were temporarily removed to the Catacombs of San Sebastiano during the mid-third-century persecutions of Valerian.

Santa Maria del Popolo

Map p. 9. Open 7–12 & 4–7, holidays 8–1.30 & 4.30–7.30. The church of Santa Maria del Popolo provides an interesting coda to the trail of St Peter, for it stands on the site of the mausoleum of the Domitii, the family of Nero, the emperor who sent Peter and Paul to their deaths. Nero's ghost was said to haunt the spot until the ground was consecrated by Pope Paschal II. The first church on this site was founded in the late eleventh century.

The present church is home to Caravaggio's great canvas of *The Crucifixion of St Peter* (1600–01), in the chapel at the end of the north aisle. The scene is dramatic, and in its day it was unusual. Instead of the conventional depiction of the saint upon his upside-down cross, the artist is preoccupied with the mechanics of getting him up there. Three strapping executioners are shown hauling the great wooden contraption into position. St Peter has been fixed to it with long nails. One executioner pulls on a rope, another holds the end of the cross, and the third heaves with his back from below. His feet are dirty and a large stone and small clods of earth are scattered beside him. He still holds the spade with which he has dug the end of the cross into the earth. Caravaggio's influence on other artists has been great. However, this work was not as completely innovative as critics sometimes give it credit for being. Fifty years previously, Michelangelo had shown St Peter's crucifixion in precisely the same way, in the Cappella Paolina in the Vatican, just beyond the Sistine Chapel (*sadly no admission to the public but you can take a vitrual tour of it on www.vatican.va: click on 'Basilicas and Papal Chapels' and then 'Pauline Chapel'*). What was new in Caravaggio's work was not the idea in itself but the zoom function: there are no extraneous details, no surrounding crowd with expressions of tortured horror to deflect our attention from the main event. The main event is the only event, and its effect is very powerful.

Opposite the *Crucifixion of St Peter* is another master work by Caravaggio, the *Conversion of St Paul*, showing the saint prostrate on the road to Damascus.

ON THE TRAIL OF ST PAUL

Be thou not ashamed of the testimony of our Lord, nor of me his
prisoner.   2 Timothy 1:8

The lines quoted above were written by St Paul to Timothy, Bishop of Ephesus, from a Roman prison, perhaps the
same Mamertine Prison in which St Peter had also been
incarcerated (*see p. 18*). Paul, as is famously known, began
life as Saul, a tent-maker, born at Tarsus, capital of the Roman province of Cilicia, in modern-day Turkey. As a young
man, he was a vigorous persecutor of Christians. We learn
in Acts 8 that he 'made havoc of the church', entering
Christian houses, making arrests and having people committed to prison. He stood approvingly by as St Stephen
was stoned. It was while en route to Damascus that he had
his life-changing vision, in the form of a blinding light and
a voice asking, 'Saul, Saul, why persecutest thou me?' The
experience made him as earnest a proselytiser of the new
religion as he had once been its scourge. He outlines what
he acknowledged as his role in Galatians 2:7: 'The gospel
of the uncircumcision was committed to me, as the gospel
of the circumcision was unto Peter.' In other words, Paul's
task was to preach to the Gentiles, as Peter preached to the
Jews. Thus it was that he set out on his missions to Greece
and Asia Minor, and finally to Rome. Paul's epistle to the
Romans clearly indicates his intention to visit them on his
way to Spain, and it appears that he did indeed do so.

The beheading of St Paul. Scene from the Pauline Door of the basilica of San Paolo fuori le Mura, sculpted by Guido Veroi (2008). The saint is depicted with the physical attributes commonly ascribed to him: thin hair on top, a pointed beard, prominent eyebrows. He kneels upon the basalt flagstones of a Roman road. An angel descends from Heaven bearing a martyr's palm.

ATTENZIONE!

AREA SOTTOPOSTA
A VIDEOSORVEGLIANZA
PER
RAGIONI DI SICUREZZA

Art. 13 del Codice in materia di protezione
dei dati personali (D.Lgs. 196/2003)

'Beware! CCTV cameras in operation for security reasons.' Notices like this are posted all along the boundary wall of the block where the Castrum Praetorium once stood, the barracks that housed the imperial bodyguard, to which St Paul was taken on arrival in Rome. It is still a high security area.

Following an uproar in Jerusalem, where certain of the Jews objected to his teaching, he was apprehended by Roman centurions. When they discovered that their prisoner was a citizen of a Roman town, they were unable, according to Roman law, to lay hands on him, for no free-born Roman could be arrested without trial. Paul was sent to Rome, to plead his innocence before the emperor Nero.

He arrived in the city along the Via Appia. On his arrival he was taken to the headquarters of the Praetorian Guard (*map p. 9*), where the Biblioteca Nazionale stands today as well as, appropriately enough, a Ministry of Defence barracks. Because Paul was a Roman citizen, he was not detained but was permitted to live apart, under guard. We know from Acts 28 that he summoned the elders of Rome's Jewish community to this guarded lodging and preached to them, 'and some believed the things which were spoken, and some believed not'. We know also that 'he dwelt two whole years in his own hired house, and received all that came in unto him, preaching the Kingdom of God, and teaching those things which concern the Lord Jesus Christ, with all confidence, no man forbidding him.'

Scripture is silent about what happened next. But he was certainly seized and placed in custody again, this time in a real gaol. From his epistles we know that some of his erstwhile followers deserted him, ashamed to be associated with a man in chains. He was martyred, according to tradition by beheading, outside the city to the south, at the place now known as Tre Fontane.

There are two churches in Rome that claim to stand on the site of Paul's lodging. Both traditions are of some antiquity, and it is conceivable that the saint had more than one dwelling place in the course of the two years that he lived here.

The dwelling places of St Paul in Rome

Remember that Jesus Christ of the seed of David was raised from the dead according to my gospel, wherein I suffer trouble as an evil doer, even unto bonds; but the word of God is not bound.   2 Timothy 2:8–9

Tucked away on one of the cobbled backstreets near Campo de' Fiori, only a few steps away from the spot on Largo Argentina where Julius Caesar was assassinated, and close to Via Arenula, the old western boundary of the

Jewish ghetto, is a small church called **San Paolo alla Regola** (*map p. 302, B3; open 5–8, Sun 6.30–8.30*). Its name is a corruption of *arenula*, from the Italian word for sand, a reference to the soft, silty soil of this part of town, so close to the Tiber, which until comparatively recently was not banked up. The area is an interesting mix, being very run-down and on the ascendant at the same time, with a brightly-lit cake shop in Via dell'Arco del Monte and silver and jewellery shops around the Monte di Pietà itself, the old pawnbroker's, where the destitute would turn in their belongings for a few pence.

San Paolo alla Regola advertises itself proudly as the 'First Residence of St Paul in Rome'. On the west wall is a Latin text referring to Paul's conversion and ministry, a paraphrase of Acts 9: 'Saul fell to the earth, and heard a voice saying unto him, Saul, Saul, why persecutest thou me? I am Jesus. And he said, Lord, what wilt thou have me to do? Arise, and go into the city, bear my name before the Gentiles, and kings, and the children of Israel.' At the end of the south aisle is a little chapel dedicated to St Paul, on the site of what by tradition is claimed to have been his lodging and the room where he taught. The wooden ceiling is very pretty, painted olive green, decorated with white palms of martyrdom and St Paul's attribute, the sword. The modern mosaic above the altar shows the saint chained, with the centurion who was set to guard him sitting bored and hangdog in the background. On either side are large stone tablets with the

St Paul is beheaded before the emperor Nero. In the background we see the saint appearing from heaven to Plautilla, to return to her the veil which he had requested as a blindfold. Plautilla was a Roman matron said to have been baptised by St Peter.

words from Acts 28 that Paul spoke to the Jewish elders, perhaps on this very spot: 'For the hope of Israel I am bound with this chain,' and a sentence from his second epistle to Timothy, written from a Roman prison: 'But the word of God is not bound.'

This latter text recurs, engraved on a column in the crypt of **Santa Maria in Via Lata**. The church stands on the busy Corso (*map p. 302, C2*). The narrowness of the pavement and the incessant hurly burly of people and traffic make it difficult to stand back to admire the façade, which in any case is besmirched with a thick layer of grime. But it is a famous work by the architect and painter Pietro da Cortona, a vertical, upthrusting arrangement of columns, broken by a Serlian window on the upper level. In the church crypt (*open Tues–Fri 4–7, Sat and Sun also 10–1, afternoon hours 3–6 in winter*) are remains of a first-century Roman building claimed as the house of St Luke and also of St Paul, where he lived under guard. We know that Paul wrote many of his epistles from Rome. It is very tempting to believe that he wrote them right here, in one of these two churches.

The road to martyrdom

Because nothing is known for certain about St Peter's time in Rome, it is impossible to say what the two great Apostles might have discussed, what disagreements they may have had, how they collaborated with each other, how their ministries overlapped, if indeed they overlapped at all. If they lived and worked here at the same time, they presumably had plenty of contact with each other. And when they were each sent to their deaths, it is reasonable to suppose that they took their leave of each other. The attractive tradition of the farewell embrace has found its way into an icon type, wherein Peter and Paul are shown with their arms around each other, a last fraternal gesture

NEI PRESSI DI QUESTO SITO
UNA DEVOTA CAPPELLINA
IN ONORE DEL SANTISSIMO CROCEFISSO
DEMOLITA AGLI ALBORI DEL SECOLO XX
PER L'ALLARGAMENTO DELLA VIA OSTIENSE
SEGNAVA IL LUOGO
DOVE SECONDO UNA PIA TRADIZIONE
I PRINCIPI DEGLI APOSTOLI PIETRO E PAOLO
VENNERO SEPARATI NELL'AVVIO
AL GLORIOSO MARTIRIO

'Near this spot, a small chapel dedicated to the Crucifixion, demolished at the beginning of the twentieth century to allow the widening of the Via Ostiense, marked the place where, according to a hallowed tradition, the princes of the apostles, Peter and Paul, were separated on the eve of their glorious martyrdom.'

and exchange of moral support as each sets off towards his place of execution. The scene of this goodbye hug has been set by the side of the Via Ostiensis (in Italian, Via Ostiense), and until the road was widened in the early twentieth century, a chapel stood there, dedicated to the

Crucifixion but known as the Cappella della Separazi-
one, the Chapel of the Separation. Its site today (*map p.
9*) is occupied by a wide, tall building plastered in yellow
ochre, with red-brick dressings around the windows and
a first-floor balcony on scrolled consoles. In memory of
the two men who may once have bidden farewell to each
other here, a copy of a little stone relief has been set up
on the street-facing wall. Next door there is a Japanese
restaurant and a shop selling industrial spare parts. The
building and those adjacent to it were once part of the
Centrale Montemartini electrical works and today the
complex houses ancient sculptures belonging to the Capitoline Museums, superbly displayed in vast turbine halls
against a backdrop of monuments of the machine age. It
is one of the best small museums in Rome (*closed Mon*).

Abbazia delle Tre Fontane

*Map p. 9. Open 9–8 or 9. Bus 716 from Teatro di Marcello (get
off at the Tintoretto/Ballarin stop, from where it is a short walk
up Via Laurentina) or Metro B to San Paolo and bus 761 from
Roccardi (just outside the metro station).*

Although St Paul is said also to have been held in the
Mamertine Prison along with St Peter (*see p. 18*), there
is another place which preserves his memory better. This
is the traditional site of his martyrdom, some way to the
south of the city off the old road to the port of Ostia, at
the place known as Tre Fontane.

The Abbazia delle Tre Fontane (Abbey of the Three Fountains) was built on the site where St Paul's severed head, bouncing three times, is said to have caused three fountains to spring up. A monastic community was established here by 641. While on a visit to Rome in 1138–40, St Bernard is believed to have received the land and its monastic buildings as a gift from Pope Innocent II.

As you approach Tre Fontane, either by bus or by car or on foot, it is difficult to imagine how it can have any atmosphere of sanctity at all, so hemmed around is it by sprawling suburbs and by the roaring Via Laurentina. But the Cistercian monks have created a haven of Trappist quietude here. You turn off the fast main road along a lane bordered with tall holm oaks, past a colossal statue of St Benedict, with his finger to his lips and the inscribed injunction *Ora et Labora* ('Pray and work'), and after a few minutes emerge at a broad car park, where the café sells refreshments and selected products of cloistered industry such as Trappist beers and eucalyptus liqueur. In front of you, beyond the gate, is a little garden with a fountain, backed by two small churches, and a third in the centre, some way further on.

The church on your left is dedicated to Sts Vincent and Anastasius (**Vincenzo e Anastasio**). It was founded in the early seventh century by Pope Honorius I, who embarked on an ambitious plan to embellish existing churches or build new ones on the sites of prominent martyrdoms. It was one of the churches visited by Sigeric, newly-appointed Archbishop of Canterbury, on his visit to Rome in 990 (*see p. 148*).

The church on the right, **Santa Maria Scala Coeli**, dates from the late sixteenth century, though it is a much older foundation. Popular tradition asserts that it stands over the burial place of thousands of Christian soldiers and their captain, St Zeno, dragooned as slaves by Diocletian to build his great thermal baths, and brought here and executed when they became too frail to work but refused to renounce their faith.

The name of the church ('Stairway to Heaven') derives from a story that St Bernard, while kneeling at an altar here and praying for the soul of a man lately deceased, had a vision of that same soul climbing up from purgatory by a heavenly ladder. The altar is now preserved in the crypt, and to the right of it is a tiny low room, a relic of the prison where St Paul is said to have been held before his execution.

The exact site of that execution is occupied by the third church, **San Paolo alle Tre Fontane**, again dating from the late sixteenth century, though the original foundation is of the fifth. Ranged along the wall opposite the entrance, enclosed in elaborate marble tabernacles, are the three fountains that are said to have sprung from the earth at each point touched by the saint's head as it fell and bounced. Their gurgling is loud in the stillness, a forceful reminder of the Bible verse about 'rivers of living water' (*John 7:38*).

The basilica of San Paolo Fuori le Mura

Map p. 9. Metro B to San Paolo or any of the buses than run down Via Ostiense. Also bus 280 from Trastevere (last stop Partigiani). Open 7–6.30; cloister open 9–1 & 3–6 except Sun.

The body of the martyred St Paul was buried in a small necropolis beside the Via Ostiensis, today the busy Via Ostiense, which leads to the coast and to Fiumicino Airport. Constantine erected a basilica over the grave site, which was consecrated c. 324. All trace of that early church has now vanished: over the years it was enlarged, embellished, sacked, damaged by earthquake, rebuilt and remodelled, until finally, in 1823, it was consumed by fire. The basilica of St Paul Outside the Walls that we see today, though it shadows the footprint of its late antique ancestor, dates in tangible form almost entirely from the nineteenth century. It is a grandiose pile, fronted by a colonnaded porch to the north and a wide columned atrium to the west. Its campanile stands tall and white like a lighthouse.

It is possible to enter the basilica by the north door, but the best and most imposing entrance is from the west. Here the church is preceded by an **atrium (1)**, arranged in the form of a parterre, with evergreen hedges and palm trees surrounded by a granite colonnade. In the centre stands a statue of a cowled St Paul holding a sword, the symbol of his martyrdom.

In front of the wide west façade of the basilica is the **Pauline Flame (2)**, first lit at Vespers during the feast of St Peter and St Paul in 2008, at the inauguration of the Pauline Year, which marked two thousand years since the saint's birth. It has remained burning ever since, and, according to the text set up beside it, 'gives light to each pilgrim who comes through the Pauline Door into the Papal Basilica of St Paul Outside the Walls to venerate the memory of the Apostle of the Gentiles'.

In around the year 1450, an English Augustinian friar by the name of John Capgrave wrote a handbook to Rome entitled *Ye Solace of Pilgrims*. In it he offers a compelling reason why San Paolo fuori le Mura should be entered by the west door:

> The altar of St Peter's church stands in the west and the altar of St Paul's church stands in the east. Some pilgrims there be that know the cause why men go in at the west end of St Paul's, for the readier way is to enter by the north side. The cause why those men that know the place enter by the west is this: for after the time that St Paul's head was smitten off two miles thence, it was carried and hidden where the west door is now and afterwards found and kept with great reverence. And in the worship of that head whosoever enters by that door has every day twenty-eight years of indulgence[5] with remission of the third part of their sins.

5   For indulgences, see p. 260.

Unless it is a Holy Year, in which case the *Porta Santa* (*see p. 88*) will be open, the **Pauline Door (3)** is that by which the public enters today. It is the work of Guido Veroi (2008) and shows scenes from the life of the saint, including his conversion and his martyrdom. Veroi (b. 1926) had hitherto been best known as a medallist. His designs include the former 500 lire piece and a commemorative 2 euro coin for the Vatican, struck in 2004.

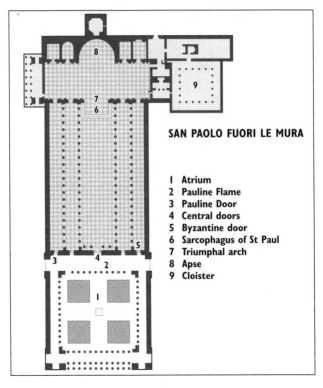

SAN PAOLO FUORI LE MURA

1 **Atrium**
2 **Pauline Flame**
3 **Pauline Door**
4 **Central doors**
5 **Byzantine door**
6 **Sarcophagus of St Paul**
7 **Triumphal arch**
8 **Apse**
9 **Cloister**

Because it is so rarely used, the **central door (4)** of the basilica tends to be overlooked, but it is artistically the finest, its two leaves meeting to form a cross, patterned like a twirling Tree of Life picked out in silver. It is the work of an artist of the Fascist era, Antonio Maraini (1886–1963), but it has none of the soulless monumentality of that time. The panels under the lateral arms of the cross show scenes from the life of St Peter (left) and of St Paul (right). The bright silver figures of Christ appearing to each Apostle, which form the central scene of both series, are particularly striking (*see illustration opposite*). From bottom to top the scenes are as follows:

- St Peter baptising
- St Peter founds the see of Rome

- Christ gives the keys to St Peter

- St Peter's vision of Christ (Domine, Quo Vadis?)
- Crucifixion of St Peter

- St Paul arrives in Rome
- St Paul in his guarded lodging

- Conversion of St Paul (Road to Damascus)

- St Paul preaches in Rome

- Beheading of St Paul

Interior of San Paolo fuori le Mura

Light is muted inside the basilica: it filters in shadowily through the alabaster windows and in clear piercing shafts from the upper clerestory. Above the colonnade runs a frieze of mosaic medallions of all the popes.

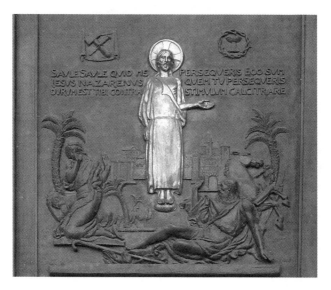

'Saul, Saul, why persecutest thou me? I am Jesus of Nazareth whom thou persecutest. It is hard for thee to kick against the goad.' Christ appears to Paul on the road to Damascus. Detail from the central door of San Paolo fuori le Mura.

At the west end, it is worth putting a coin in the light-box to see the lovely **Byzantine door (5)**, made in Constantinople in 1070 and consisting of fifty-four bronze panels inlaid with silver. The panels are arranged in three groups of twelve: on the left-hand door, from the top, are twelve scenes from the life of Christ, from the Nativity to Pentecost. These are followed by a Cross and a dedicatory inscription, and then twenty-four scenes of the apostles

Above left: The martyrdom of St Paul. Above right: St Paul with Christ. Panels from the bronze Byzantine door of San Paolo fuori le Mura, made in 1070.

and their martyrdoms, covering the remainder of the left-hand door and part of the right. A panel representing Moses is separated from panels of eleven prophets by another Cross and a dedicatory inscription. In each bottom corner is a Byzantine eagle.

In the confessio beneath high altar, below a casket containing a fragment of chain, can be seen the rough stone side of the **sarcophagus of St Paul (6)**, behind a metal grille fashioned to look like knotted rope. Forensic examination in 2009 resulted in the conclusion that these were indeed the relics of St Paul, the mortal remains of the man whose 'letters were weighty and powerful but whose bodily presence was weak' (*2 Corinthians 10*), who is said to have been small and bandy-legged, with knobbly knees and sparse hair, a pointed black beard and eyebrows meeting in the middle over keen grey eyes.

The **mosaic decoration on the triumphal arch (7)** dates originally from the fifth century, though it has been almost entirely reworked since then. A stern Christ is flanked by the symbols of the Evangelists and the twenty-four elders of the Apocalypse, who fall down and wor-

Interior view of San Paolo fuori le Mura. It follows the same plan as the original basilica before the fire of 1823: a wide nave separated from the aisles by a round-arched colonnade, with a clerestory above and a frieze with roundels of the popes. Mosaics adorn the apse and triumphal arch.

ship and cast their crowns before the throne (*Revelation 4:10*). Below the elders, to right and left, are the figures of St Paul and St Peter. Paul has the gammadia L and Θ (*see p. 175*).

The **apse mosaic (8)** is very fine, the work of Venetian mosaicists of the early thirteenth century, though much restored after the 1823 fire. It shows Christ flanked by St Paul and St Luke. Luke, who wrote the Acts of the Apostles as well as his own Gospel, was known personally to St Paul. In 2 Timothy 4, written from his Roman prison, Paul remarks ruefully that 'Demas has forsaken me, having loved this present world, and is departed unto Thessalonica; Crescens to Galatia; Titus unto Dalmatia. Only Luke is with me.'[6] On either side of the central figures are Sts Peter and Andrew, the two fisherman brothers. The tiny donor pope is Honorius III. Below are two angels flanked by Apostles and Evangelists holding scrolls inscribed with lines from the *Gloria: Glorificamus te* (Philip); *Laudamus te* (James); *Adoramus te* (Bartholomew); *Gratias agimus tibi* (Thomas). Between the angels are a jewelled cross and symbols of the Passion.

The **cloister (9)** (*entry fee*) dates from the twelfth to the thirteenth centuries and is very beautiful, similar in design to that of St John Lateran and the work of the same craftsmen, the Vassalletti. Pairs of columns of different

6   There are claims that the house of St Luke lies under the church of Santa Maria in Via Lata (*see pp. 39–40*).

designs, straight, twisted and spiralling, some with Cosmatesque decoration, enclose a garden of palms, roses, box hedges and a fountain. Fragments of funerary monuments and inscriptions, both pagan and Christian, are arranged around the walks. The pagan ones begin with the letters D.M. standing for '*Dis Manibus*', commending the deceased to the spirits of the dead. They often have depressions or holes for libations to be poured into the grave. The early Christian inscriptions, either in Latin or Greek, are accompanied by familiar symbols such as the dove, ivy leaf, anchor or Chi Rho (*see p. 108*).

Santa Maria del Popolo

Map p. 9. Open 7–12 & 4–7, holidays 8–1.30 & 4.30–7.30.
This church has no connection to the historical St Paul, nor to his legend. However, it does contain one of the greatest works of art in all Rome, Caravaggio's splendid canvas of St Paul's conversion on the road to Damascus in the chapel at the end of the north aisle. It hangs opposite the *Crucifixion of St Peter* (*see pp. 32–33*). An elderly carter and his horse are shown picking their way carefully over the sprawled figure of Paul, who lies helpless in the road, dressed in a Roman soldier's garb, his arms bathed in the radiance of his vision, which also glances off the flank of the horse.

THE PAPAL BASILICAS & PILGRIMAGE CHURCHES

'Basilica' was the name given in ancient Rome to a large public administrative building. Typically, a basilica would be raised on a stepped platform and its main entrance would be approached under a columned entrance portico. The interior space was divided by colonnades and terminated at the far end in an apse, where the judge or magistrate or presiding official would sit. In front of this was a wide space which could accommodate a great number of people. For Christians, whose system of worship—unlike that of the pagan gods—was congregational, this design held appeal. It provided plenty of room for the faithful to attend services, without any attendant

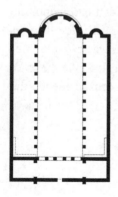

Plan of a typical basilica, a Roman administrative building adapted for Christian liturgical use. The interior space is divided into nave and aisles, and terminates in a central apse, where the clergy's semicircular throne would have been. Typically there are five entrance doors, under the entrance porch or narthex, of which one is the Porta Santa or Holy Door. For more on Holy Doors, see p. 88.

association with the old state religion: basilicas had been civic spaces, not places of cult. Thus it was that the basilica plan was adopted by the early Christians for their churches: preceded by an entrance porch, the Christian basilica was divided in the interior into nave and aisles, and it terminated at its far end in an apse where the bishop had his throne, flanked by the synthronon, a semicircular bench for the clergy.

In the year 313, the year in which he passed his edict granting freedom of worship to Christians, the emperor Constantine set in hand the building of basilicas in Rome, expressly to be used as churches by members of the newly-liberated faith. Before this time, there had been no fixed places of cult and the Christian communities had met in each other's houses. The first Christian basilica to be built, in direct imitation of the great civic constructions of the ancient city, was St John Lateran.

THE PAPAL BASILICAS

The four principal basilica-churches in Rome are St John Lateran, St Peter's, San Paolo fuori le Mura and Santa Maria Maggiore. Known as patriarchal basilicas until 2006, when Pope Benedict XVI relinquished the title of Patriarch of the West, they now go by the name of papal basilicas. They are not the same as the pilgrimage churches (*see p. 92*), though they do form part of that group.

ST JOHN LATERAN

Map p. 303, F4. Bus 117 from Piazza del Popolo and the Colosseum. Open 7–6.30; cloisters open 9–6. There are public toilets in the basilica, entered from the north aisle under the monument to Cardinal Caracciolo.

Around the busy Piazza di San Giovanni in Laterano are assembled some of the most important monuments in Christian history, including the first church of Rome. The obelisk, the tallest in the world, dates from the fifteenth century BC. It was brought to Rome from Egypt in the fourth century, was placed in the Circus Maximus, and then moved here in 1588. The Latin inscription on its base reads: 'Constantine, victor in Christ, baptised on this spot by St Sylvester, propagated the glory of the Cross'.

The inscription, unfortunately, cannot be taken as reflecting fact on any level. Constantine was indeed victorious over his rival emperor Maxentius, at the Battle of the Milvian Bridge to the north of the modern city centre, in 312. According to the much-repeated legend, he had a dream on the eve of the battle in which he saw a bright cross with the words: *In hoc signo vinces*: 'By this sign you will conquer'. Constantine did win, and his armies thenceforth fought under the standard of the Cross, the labarum. But whether Constantine truly considered himself to have been victorious in Christ is a matter open to serious debate. This victory, rather, was one stage on his path to conversion: it was not the final step. Constantine was not baptised on this spot[7], nor anywhere near it. He received the sacrament only very shortly before his death, at Nicomedia in 337, and the cleric who baptised him was not Pope Sylvester, who died in 335.

The importance of the baptistery of St John Lateran as the earliest place where Roman Christians were received into an officially sanctioned faith is nevertheless beyond dispute. It is also very beautiful.

The foundation of St John Lateran

The basilica of St John Lateran is the cathedral of Rome (*Omnium urbis et orbis Ecclesiarum Mater et Caput*: 'the mother and head of all the churches of the city and the world'). It derives its name from the patrician family of Plautius Lateranus, whose house and land were seized after his implication in a plot to murder the emperor Nero in AD 65. The property passed to Constantine as the dowry of his wife Fausta, and Constantine decreed that the land should be used to build a church for the see of Rome. This is the earliest Christian basilica in the city.

Nothing remains of the original early fourth-century foundation, nor of the later, much embellished church which Dante saw and from whose loggia Pope Boniface VIII proclaimed the first Holy Year in 1300. That church

7 The cherished legend of Constantine's Roman baptism can be followed in a charming series of frescoes in the nearby convent of the Santi Quattro Coronati (*see p. 134*).

was consumed by fire in 1308, and over the years since then its successor has been enlarged and rebuilt, beautified and refurbished, so that what you see today is almost entirely the product of the seventeenth to the nineteenth centuries.

The palace which adjoins the basilica was the original seat of the papal court. Between 1309 and 1377 the popes ruled from Avignon (in France today, though at the time it was in papal territory). After their return to Rome, they set up court in the Vatican, but their coronation ceremonies continued to be held at St John Lateran until 1870, when Rome fell to the Italian national armies and the pontiffs were confined to the Vatican City. Under the Lateran Treaty of 11th February 1929, this basilica, with those of San Paolo fuori le Mura and Santa Maria Maggiore, was accorded the privilege of 'extraterritoriality', meaning that although it is not within the geographical limits of the Vatican state, it is subject to Vatican jurisdiction.

What to see
The central portal of the main entrance front (1) is filled with the ancient bronze doors of the Curia, the senate house in the Roman Forum. They were moved here in the seventeenth century by Pope Alexander VII. On the left is a statue of Constantine, restored in parts, from his baths (no longer extant) on the Quirinal Hill.

The design of the interior preserves the lines of the re-modelling by Bernini's great rival Borromini in 1646–49. He

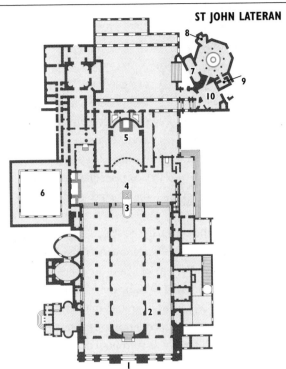

ST JOHN LATERAN

<u>**BASILICA**</u>
1 Doors from the ancient Senate House
2 Fresco of Pope Boniface VIII proclaiming the first Holy Year
3 Tomb of Pope Martin V
4 Papal altar
5 Apse
6 Cloister

<u>**BAPTISTERY**</u>
7 Chapel of Sts Cyprian and Justina
8 Chapel of St John the Baptist
9 Chapel of St John the Evangelist
10 Chapel of St Venantius

Pope Boniface VIII on the loggia of St John Lateran, proclaiming the Holy Year of 1300. Fresco by Giotto.

designed the niches between the massive nave piers, each of which contains a colossal statue of an apostle. The ceiling is older (1566), and the marble Cosmatesque floor dates from the fifteenth century.

On the first nave pier on the south side **(2)** there is a fresco fragment detached from the loggia of the old basilica showing Pope Boniface VIII proclaiming the Holy Year of 1300 (*for more on this, see p. 74*). The work is believed to be by the hand of Giotto. Pope Boniface was an unlovable character in many ways, but he seems to have had an appreciation of the arts. Vasari tells the story of how Giotto was summoned to Rome[8]:

[The papal messenger] declared the purpose of the pope, and the manner in which that pontiff desired to avail himself of his assistance, and finally, requested to have a drawing, that he might send it to his holiness. Giotto, who was very courteous, took a

8   Quoted in the notes to Longfellow's translation of Dante's *Purgatorio*, 1867.

sheet of paper, and a pencil dipped in a red colour; then, resting his elbow on his side to form a sort of compass, with one turn of the hand he drew a circle, so perfect and exact that it was a marvel to behold. This done, he turned smiling to the courtier saying,

'Here is your drawing.'

'Am I to have nothing more than this?' inquired the latter, conceiving himself to be jested with.

'That is enough and to spare,' returned Giotto, 'Send it with the rest and you will see if it will be recognised.'

It was. Giotto was invited to Rome, we are told, where his talents were appreciated and where he was treated very honourably.

In the confessio is the bronze tomb-slab of Martin V (d. 1431) **(3)**. It has become a custom to toss coins down onto the effigy-in-relief of the Roman pope who healed the Great Western Schism. For much of the fourteenth century, the popes had had their seat not in Rome but in Avignon (*see p. 58*). Pope Gregory XI, though a French-man, had brought his court and curia back to Rome, partly in response to the pleas of St Catherine of Siena. But division and strife still reigned within the Church, with rival claimants to the tiara being nominated supreme pontiff by opposing factions of cardinals. It was not until the Roman-born Oddone Colonna was elected in 1417,

taking the regnal name of Martin V, that the rift was finally healed. Pope Martin's burial here has a slight piquancy
to it, because although he restored papal dignity to his native city, the popes were never again to have their seat in
the Lateran. In the years of the so-called 'Babylonian cap-
tivity', when the popes had been in Avignon, the basilica
and palace had fallen into disrepair and on their return to
Rome, the popes chose an alternative seat on the Vatican
Hill next to St Peter's, in a house which had previously
been used to accommodate visiting dignitaries. Pope Martin returned to the Lateran, however, to be buried.

The Gothic baldachin above the papal altar **(4)** contains nineteenth-century reliquaries said to contain the
heads of St Peter and St Paul. The heads were brought
here in 1369, in a bid to make the Lateran the equal of St
Peter's for holy associations. The altar, reconstructed by
Pius IX, encloses part of a wooden table (not visible) at
which St Peter is alleged to have celebrated Mass.

The apse **(5)** is a late nineteenth-century reconstitution
of the thirteenth-century original from the time of Pope
Nicholas IV (under whom the apse mosaic of Santa Maria
Maggiore was also made by the same mosaicist, Jacopo
Torriti). The original must have been very fine. The central figure, flanked by the Virgin and St John, is the Cross.
From out of the heavens, below the head of Christ, the
dove of the Holy Spirit lets flow from its beak a fountain of water, which falls upon a hill on which the Cross
stands and from which four rivers gush downwards to

the sea, watering deer and sheep and flowers. The sea is inhabited by aquatic creatures and human figures, one with a water jar, another casting a fishing net. Under the Cross, upon the branches of a palm tree, stands the phoenix, symbol of resurrection. Pope Nicholas, clad in a red robe, kneels at the feet of the Virgin.

The cloister

The beautiful cloister **(6**; *entrance fee*), with grass and olive trees in the centre, is the masterpiece of Jacopo and Pietro Vassalletto (c. 1222–32). The columns, some plain and some twisted, are adorned with Cosmatesque mosaic. Many interesting fragments from the ancient basilica are displayed around the walks.

THE LATERAN BAPTISTERY

Map p. 303, F4. Open 7–12.30 & 4–7.30.
The basilica of St John Lateran has a dual dedication, to St John the Evangelist (St John the Divine) and St John the Baptist. The baptistery, logically, is dedicated to the latter. It stands on land that had belonged to Constantine's wife Fausta, and remains of an imperial-era *domus* and a nymphaeum or bath-house have been found here. There were water-conduits already *in situ*, therefore, which would have ensured a plentiful supply to the baptismal immersion tank. Although the baptistery was built by Constantine c. 315–24, it was not, despite legends to the contrary,

the scene of his baptism as the first Christian emperor. It may, more nefariously, be the scene of Fausta's death. She was suffocated in her bath in 326, in circumstances that remain unclear. Had Constantine ordered her murder, on charges of adultery? Or had Fausta taken her own life, on finding that she was pregnant with another man's child? Or something entirely different? Neither tradition nor scholarship have revealed the answer.

The baptismal pool

The entrance to the baptistery is by the north door, which leads from Piazza di San Giovanni. The door is not part of the original design; it was added by Pope Gregory XIII for the Holy Year of 1575, to ease the flow of pilgrims through the restricted space. Baptisms take place in the central pool, which is surrounded by eight columns of porphyry, gifts from Constantine to the builders of the first baptistery here. Originally the pool would have had water in it; candidates for baptism would have entered the building by the south door and walked through the baptismal pool from south to north. Today the water is contained in the green basalt font, a basin from an ancient Roman bath, its sides carved with stylised ivy leaves inside rings, symbols of faith and eternity. The seventeenth-century bronze reliefs on the font cover show Christ being baptised by St John and Constantine being baptised by Pope Sylvester (*for Constantine's baptism, see p. 57*). Around the drum of the domical vault are modern copies of seventeenth-century paintings by Andrea Sacchi (who lies buried in the basilica), showing scenes from the life of John the Baptist. On the architrave above the eight porphyry columns are Latin couplets, inscribed here by Pope Sixtus III (432–40), who incorporated the gifted columns into the baptistery design, turning it from a circular building into an octagonal one. The poem forms a meditation on baptism, grace and salvation and can be translated roughly thus:

From this divine seed is born a people worthy to be
    sanctified, born of water by the fecund Spirit.
Sinner, to be purified, immerse yourself in the sacred
    flood. The water receives you old and will restore
    you new.
No division exists between those who are thus
    reborn: one font, one spirit, one faith unites them.
Our Mother Church gives virgin birth in this water
    to those who are quickened by the breath of God.
If you wish to be stainless, wash yourself in this pool,
    whether burdened by original sin or by your own.
This font is life and washes all the world, taking its
    origin from the wounds of Christ.
Your hope is in heaven, you who are reborn here;
    eternal life does not await those born but once.
Let neither the number of your sins nor their nature
    deter you: all who are born in this stream will be
    saved.

The side chapels

Four lateral chapels lead off the baptistery. The only one that is contemporary with the central core of the building is the **Chapel of St Cyprian and St Justina (7)**, for this was the original entrance. Its elongated shape, rounded at both ends, is the same as the narthex of Santa Costanza (*see p. 177*), a building of roughly the same date. Originally it would have acted as a sort of holding area for those waiting their turn to be baptised. The altar on the left as you enter the chapel has an altarpiece of the *Martyrdom of Sts Cyprian and Justina*, two early fourth-century saints from Phrygia. Above it is a very beautiful fifth-century mosaic, with curling acanthus fronds against a deep blue ground and at the top a circlet of doves and jewelled crosses. The acanthus, always a popular decorative motif in pagan Roman art, was adapted in early Christianity as a symbol of eternal life. The chapel opposite honours the third-century virgin martyrs Rufina and Secunda. The rear door of the chapel, the original baptistery entrance, is flanked by two splendid, huge antique columns supporting a fine Roman architrave (visible through the glass panels).

The **Chapel of St John the Baptist (8)** was built by Pope Hilarius (461–68). Behind a grille it preserves its original doors, inscribed in Latin with a text identifying Hilarius as their donor ('Offered by Bishop Hilarius, servant of Christ, in honour of St John the Baptist'). The doors are famous for the musical sound they produce when pushed open—sadly nowadays there is an outer grille in front of them, which tends to be locked. The architrave above the two porphyry columns that flank the entrance bears a Latin text from the book of Isaiah: *Erunt aspera in vias planas*: 'The rough places shall be made plain'. The companion chapel, the **Chapel of St John the Evangelist (9)**, was also built by Pope Hilarius, though the doors are later, from the twelfth century. The inscription on the architrave reads: *Diligite alterutrum*: 'Love one another', an exhortation that is repeated in St John's first and second epistles. The vault of the ceiling is covered by a lovely golden mosaic with a central Agnus Dei and vases of flowers and birds around the edges.

The **Chapel of St Venantius (10)** was added in 640 by Pope John IV, a native of Dalmatia, to house the relics of certain Dalmatian saints, including the martyred bishop Venantius. Work was completed by John's successor, Pope Theodore I (642–49), who commissioned the mosaics in the apse and on the triumphal arch. The bust of Christ is flanked by angels. Below them are ranged eight saints on either side of the praying Madonna (difficult to see because of the top of the altar). The saint on the far left, carrying a model of the chapel, is Pope Theodore; that on the far right is Pope John IV. To the left and right of the Virgin are Sts Peter and Paul, flanked in turn by St John the Baptist and St John the Evangelist. The Baptist, the Evangelist and St Paul all have gammadia on their vestments; the two former an H, while Paul has a P (*for more on gammadia, see p. 175*). On the triumphal arch are more saints, with the symbols of the Evangelists and the holy cities of Bethlehem and Jerusalem. Remains of second-century Roman baths built above a first-century villa, with a mosaic pavement, are preserved at both sides of the chapel.

THE SCALA SANTA, SANCTA SANCTORUM & TRIBUNE

On the east side of Piazza di San Giovanni stands a plain white building, constructed in the late sixteenth century to house the stairway of the old Lateran Palace, which in the previous century had been declared to be a great and holy relic: no less than the very stairway of Pilate's house, down which Christ descended after his condemnation. This **Scala Santa** or 'Holy Stair' (*open 6.15–12 & 3–6.15, or 3.30–6.45 in summer*) consists of twenty-eight steps of Tyrian marble, now protected by wooden boards. Worshippers may only ascend them on their knees. The old wooden planks creak as they do so, like the weathered timbers of an old ship rocking on a calm sea.

At the top of the steps (also accessible by side staircases, which you may ascend on foot) is the chapel of the **Sancta Sanctorum**, the holy of holies, the former private chapel of the pope. The chapel and its decoration date from the late thirteenth century (*to enquire about guided visits, T: 06 7726 6641; scalasanta@scalasanta.org*).

Through thickly barred windows you can view it. A Latin text proclaims, 'There is no holier place in all the world'. Its special sanctity is conferred by an ancient icon of Christ, thickly encased in silver, said to be the work of St Luke guided by an angel, hence its name *Acheiropoieton* ('made without hands'). Other precious artefacts once housed here are now in the Vatican Museums.

Around the corner of the Scala Santa to the southeast is the **Tribune**, built in the mid-eighteenth century and decorated with copies of the mosaics from the dining hall of the old Lateran Palace, which was built by Leo III for the celebration of state banquets. In the centre is Christ sending the Apostles to preach the Gospel. On the right, St Peter gives the papal stole to Leo III and the banner of Christianity to Charlemagne. Both Leo and Charlemagne

Detail of the mosaic Tribune, showing Christ presenting the labarum (the standard of the Cross) to Constantine. Constantine adopted the labarum as his military ensign, and enemy armies are said to have developed a superstitious terror of it. Whether his adoption of the symbol was directly related to his vision on the eve of the Battle of the Milvian Bridge (AD 312), when he saw a flaming Cross and the words 'By this sign you shall conquer', is a matter of scholarly dispute.

have square haloes, indicating that they were alive at the time the original mosaic was made. On the left, Christ is seen giving the keys to Pope Sylvester (as successor to St Peter) and the labarum, or standard of the Cross, to Constantine.

ST PETER'S BASILICA

Map p. 300, B2. Open 7–6.30 (until 6pm in Oct–March). Entrance is free. The basilica is often crowded and you may have to stand in line for as long as 30mins waiting to get in. You will be asked to put your bag through a security check. Parts of the basilica are often closed at short notice and the vergers can be gruff and unaccommodating. The east end is usually closed to casual visitors, being reserved for those attending Mass.

On Sundays at noon, when the pope is in Rome, he appears at his window in the Vatican Palace to bless the crowd in the square below. Audiences are given on Wednesdays, either in the Audience Hall or in St Peter's Square itself. For more details, see p. 235.

For all up-to-date information (things are apt to change at short notice), see www.vatican.va, which also has details of the divine services at which the pope will officiate (click on 'Liturgical Celebrations').

The approach to St Peter's (Ponte Sant'Angelo)

By far the finest way to approach St Peter's is across Ponte

Sant'Angelo. This pedestrian bridge was built by Hadrian in AD 134 as an approach to his mausoleum on the further bank of the Tiber. The mausoleum still stands: it is now the fortress-museum of Castel Sant'Angelo, where the medieval and Renaissance popes stored their ammunition and their treasury, where prisoners languished in irons at His Holiness's pleasure, and where the pontiff would retreat in times of danger or civil unrest.

If the crowds on the bridge are thick, imagine yourself as a medieval pilgrim; for in those days, especially in Holy Years, the crush of the faithful hastening to St Peter's was intense and on one occasion, in 1450, a shying mule caused pandemonium on the bridge and several hundred people were crushed to death. If you are fortunate, things will be quieter than that and you will be able to cross the bridge at leisure, admiring the angel statues on the parapets, designed by Bernini and sculpted by him and his assistants.

As you approach the bridge from the south, you will notice that it is sternly guarded by the apostles Peter and Paul, whose statues stand on the site of two demolished chapels that had been built to commemorate the disaster of 1450. St Paul stands on the right, and the Latin inscription on his plinth reads, 'Whence cometh punishment for the proud'. On the left is St Peter, with an accompanying inscription reading, 'Whence cometh reward for the meek'. After this comes the procession of angels, each one holding an instrument of the Passion as follows:

Left parapet (west)	Right parapet (east)
The Scourge: 'I am ready for the scourge.'	**The Column:** 'My throne on a column.'
The Crown of Thorns: 'In my affliction they stabbed me with thorns.'	**The Cloth of Veronica:** Inscription missing.
The Garments and Dice: 'They drew lots over my garments.'	**The Nails:** 'They turned their gaze upon him whom they crucified.'
The Titulus: 'God reigned upon the wood.'	**The Cross:** 'His kingdom upon his shoulders.'
The Sponge: 'They gave me vinegar to drink.'	**The Lance:** 'You wounded my heart.'

St Peter's Square

St Peter's Square, an elliptical space girded on two sides by a colonnade, forms the atrium to St Peter's basilica. It is a masterpiece of urban planning by the great Baroque sculptor and architect Gian Lorenzo Bernini. The design is thought to have been modelled on that at the Forum of Constantine in Constantinople. Here the crowd gathers on Sunday at noon to receive the papal blessing (*see p. 84*) and on Wednesdays in fine weather, when the pope gives an audience in the open air.

The colonnades (each one a fourfold enfilade of columns) give onto a trapezoidal space before the basilica steps. When viewed from above or on a map (*p. 300, C2*), the whole design has the shape of a keyhole, entirely appropriate for the apostle to whom the keys of Heaven were entrusted.

A total of a hundred and forty statues of saints and martyrs surmounts the colonnades and basilica forecourt. In the centre of the elliptical part of the square are two fountains and an obelisk, the latter originally from Alexandria and brought in AD 37 to adorn the Circus of Caligula (later known as the Circus of Nero, where St Peter was crucified; *see plan on p. 31*). Between the obelisk and each fountain, set into the paving, is a circle of porphyry. Standing and looking at the colonnades from these points, it will appear that the four rows of columns are in fact one. This fact has entered the repertoire of soundbites regularly relayed to tourist groups. You can sometimes see guides, furled umbrella held aloft, attempting to get each member of her flock clustered around the porphyry disc. It won't work. You really do have to be absolutely on the disc before the optical illusion can take effect.

The porch of St Peter's

Fixed high up on the wall to the right of the entrance door is a stone plaque inscribed with the text of the bull of Boniface VIII, *Antiquorum habet*, which proclaimed the first Holy Year in 1300 (*see below*).

POPE BONIFACE VIII & THE FIRST HOLY YEAR

The three main pilgrimage destinations in the medieval Christian world were Rome, Santiago de Compostela and Jerusalem, all of them holy cities where the faithful came in search of relics and to behold the places where saints had lived and where miracles had been performed. They came, in other words, in search of tangible confirmations of their faith. They also came to gain temporal remission for their sins.

Though Rome had been a popular place of pilgrimage since 640, after Jerusalem fell to the sword of Islam, its status changed dramatically in the year 1300, when, on 22nd February, Pope Boniface VIII, a worldling, a lawyer and a resolute champion of papal supremacy, instituted what came to be known as the first Holy Year or Jubilee, promising plenary indulgences to all those who visited the basilicas of St Peter and St Paul. Rome witnessed a flock of incomers such as had never been known before, not even in the days of the old pagan emperors. Plenary indulgences had hitherto been obtainable only by crusaders or pilgrims to the Holy Land. Pope Boniface was making them available to a whole new swathe of Christendom. The text of Boniface's bull reads thus:

'In order that the blessed apostles Peter and Paul may be more widely honoured, by the fact that the basilicas of these same apostles shall be more piously frequented by the faithful, and in order also that the faithful may feel their strength renewed by the favour of special gifts, We, by grace of almighty God and trusting in the authority and merits of these same apostles, and by virtue of the counsel of our brethren and of the plenitude of our apostolic power, in the present year, the thirteen hundredth so lately begun since the birth of our Lord Jesus Christ, and for every hundredth year in the future, do grant the following: that on all those who enter with reverence into these basilicas, repenting sincerely and being confessed, and likewise also on all those who shall repent sincerely and shall be confessed thereafter, on all these, we say, shall be conferred the remission, not only full but even absolute, of all their sins.'

A full and absolute pardon for all one's sins is a tempting idea and many were tempted, flocking to Rome on pilgrimage to the two basilicas. The custom of Holy Years has been kept up ever since. The interval between them was reduced from a hundred years to thirty-three (the lifetime of Christ) in 1343, and in the following century it was reduced further, to twenty-five years. This quarter-century interval has been maintained ever since: the most recent Holy Year was in 2000; the next will be 2025. The door to the right of the plaque is the Porta Santa, the door which is kept open in Holy Years (*see p. 88*).

The beautiful central door to the left of the entrance was made in the 1430s by the Florentine sculptor and architect Filarete. It has detailed bronze reliefs of the martyrdoms of St Peter and St Paul. For a description of the former, see the caption to the illustration opposite. The latter is reproduced on p. 39. The door is one of the few works of art salvaged from the old St Peter's, the church which began life as a basilica built over the grave of St Peter, and which was the scene of Charlemagne's coronation as Emperor of the Romans by Pope Leo III in 800. That basilica had fallen into such disrepair by the mid-1400s that it was taken down and a new church begun, larger and yet more sumptuous. Just how large and sumptuous it would become, by the time it was finally consecrated in 1626, had certainly never been foreseen by the pope who commissioned it, Nicholas V, despite the fact that it was he who had begun the embellishment of the papal residence in the Vatican and it was he who articulated the firm and unequivocal belief that people's faith was apt to waver 'unless they are moved by extraordinary sights'. By the time Leon Battista Alberti, Bramante, Raphael and Michelangelo, some of the greatest artists that Christendom has produced, had finished with it, the basilica of St Peter was an 'extraordinary sight' indeed.

Interior of St Peter's

On entering St Peter's, one is struck every time by the sheer immensity of the place, and by the sober grey of the

The Crucifixion of St Peter, shown in bronze relief in one of the panels of the basilica's central doors. The emperor Nero sits watching the scene from a loggia. Beside him flows the Tiber, with, on its other bank, Roman sepulchral pyramids, a terebinth tree which allegedly grew there and, anachronistically, Hadrian's Mausoleum (Castel Sant'Angelo).

fluted pilasters contrasting with the sumptuous coloured marbles. The first aisle chapel on the left is the Baptistery **(1)**, where an upturned Roman sarcophagus lid serves as the font. Some scholars believe that this is the very lid which once closed over the ashes of Hadrian in Castel Sant'Angelo, his mausoleum.

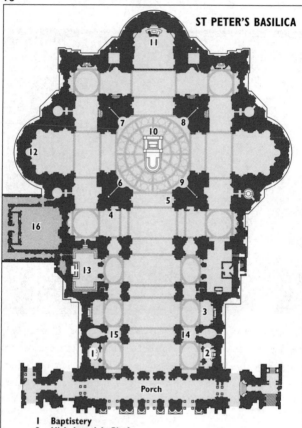

ST PETER'S BASILICA

1 Baptistery
2 Michelangelo's *Pietà*
3 Tomb of Bl. John Paul II
4 Altar of the Transfiguration (tomb of Bl. Innocent XI)
5 Statue of St Peter
6 Pier of St Andrew (entrance to the Tombs of the Popes)
7 Pier of St Veronica
8 Pier of St Helen
9 Pier of St Longinus
10 High altar (tomb of St Peter below)
11 Throne of St Peter
12 Altar of St Joseph (relics of St Simon and St Jude)
13 Cappella del Coro
14 Monument to Christina of Sweden
15 Monument to James Stuart, the Old Pretender
16 Treasury

In the first aisle chapel on the right there is invariably a crowd in front of Michelangelo's lovely *Pietà* (1499) **(2)**, carved when he was just twenty-four years old. Beyond it, further along the south aisle, is the Chapel of St Sebastian, protected by wooden barriers and an attendant verger, whose job is to stop casual tourists with their cameras and their frivolous curiosity from entering the place that is reserved for prayer, in front of the tomb of the Blessed Pope John Paul II **(3)**, whose mortal remains are marked with a simple white slab. On his death in 2005 Pope John Paul was laid to rest in the basilica crypt, but was transferred here in 2011, in time for his beatification ceremony.

The transferral involved the removal of the tomb of Innocent XI, himself a beatified pope. Pope Innocent is famed in Austria and Hungary as the instigator of the Holy League which banded together to halt the Ottomans' advance and drive them from the gates of Vienna. Malodorous rumours that he lent financial support to the Glorious Revolution in England and the Protestant succession to the throne there, have clouded his reputation, at least in Catholic circles. His monument is in the north aisle and his body now sleeps nearby, in a glass casket under the altarpiece of the Transfiguration **(4)**, a mosaic-copy of a painting by Raphael which was left unfinished on his death and which was stolen by Napoleon in 1797. Restored to Rome, it is now in the Vatican Museums.

Placed against one of the piers supporting the great dome is a much-venerated bronze statue of St Peter **(5)**.

Made in the late thirteenth century, it is a relic from old basilica. His right hand is raised in blessing and he holds the heavenly keys in his left. It is a custom to rub (or kiss) the foot of the statue, which is polished to a high shine as a result, and at busy times you see people queuing to do this while friends and family members hold cameras at the ready. On the feast day of St Peter and St Paul, 29th June, the statue is dressed in full pontifical garb.

Michelangelo's soaring central dome rests on four huge piers dedicated to St Andrew **(6)**, St Veronica **(7)**, St Helen **(8)** and St Longinus **(9)**. The entrance to the Tombs of the Popes (*see below*) opens from the pier of St Andrew. In the pier of St Veronica are kept three precious relics, shown only in Holy Week. These are the tip of the lance that pierced Christ's side, the cloth of Veronica with Christ's visage imprinted upon it, and a piece of the True Cross brought by St Helen from Jerusalem. The head of St Andrew (brother of St Peter) was formerly among the relics, but it is now in the cathedral of Patras, Greece.

Beneath the high altar is the tomb of St Peter **(10)**, around which lamps are kept perpetually lit. The altar is surmounted by a huge baldachin made by Bernini from bronze sheets removed from the porch ceiling of the Pantheon. The baldachin has the dove of the Holy Spirit on its underside and the bees of the Barberini coat of arms, the family of Pope Urban VIII under whom it was made, on its barley-twist columns. The tomb of St Peter lies directly below this altar. It can be difficult to approach the area, because the basilica is usually crowded, and every member of the crowd has a camera and is taking photographs. Your only realistic weapon is patience. Lamps are kept perpetually burning around the confessio, which announces itself as: *Sacra beati Petri confessio a Pavlo Papa V eius servo exornata 1615*, 'The holy confessio of St Peter, adorned by his servant Pope Paul V, 1615.' You can peer down into it, but there is little to see: a casket and a mosaic of Christ with his hand raised in blessing. Behind this mosaic is a niche, part of the Tropaion of Gaius, a memorial erected over the tomb in the year 160, against a red wall on which was found the inscription 'Peter' in Greek.

The tomb can be better appreciated from beneath the basilica, in the undercroft known as the **Tombs of the Popes** (*Tombe dei Papi; entrance by the pier of St Andrew under the dome; unfortunately when the basilica is very crowded, it is often closed*). People's footfalls seem hushed down here, in the strange, almost underwater atmosphere, where visitors walk the corridors lined with the sarcophagi of a jumbled assortment of popes, all to the tune of piped sacred music and noisy recorded exhortations to silence in five European languages. Here, behind glass, you can see the mosaic of Christ from slightly closer quarters. But if you really want to get near to St Peter's burial place, you must book a tour of the old street of tombs. Be warned: this requires advance planning, a lot of time, and even more persistence. For information and a description of the street of tombs, see p. 30.

Mass is frequently held at the basilica's east end. Those who attend it are able to appreciate Bernini's theatrical composition of the Throne of St Peter **(11)**, borne aloft on gilt stucco clouds which billow upwards into a burst of light, with gilded rays and a swarm of angels surrounding a window of orange glass, at the centre of which is the dove of the Holy Spirit. The sombre figures on either side of the throne are the Doctors of the Latin and Greek churches, St Augustine and St Ambrose (wearing mitres) and St Athanasius and St John Chrysostom. In the niches at either side, almost presumptuously, are the competingly magnificent tombs of Paul III (left; d. 1549) and Urban VIII (right; d. 1644, by Bernini).

The altar at the end of the north transept is dedicated to St Joseph **(12)**. In an antique porphyry sarcophagus beneath the altar are the relics of two of the apostles, St Simon and St Jude, who according to tradition were martyred together in Persia. Their relics were brought here in the seventh or eighth century. Simon is the apostle referred to as Simon the Canaanite by St Mark and St Matthew and as Simon the Zealot by St Luke. Jude (Thaddaeus), the brother of James, may possibly be identified with the author of the Epistle of Jude, whose brother James was Bishop of Jerusalem (perhaps one and the same as the apostle James the Less, whose relics are in the church of the Santi Apostoli; *see p. 166*). The Epistle of Jude is a short encyclical letter of exhortation, urging all who read it to be on their guard against those who are perverting the fledgling churches' course, against 'men who slander what they do not understand', 'shepherds who feed only themselves', and 'grumblers and fault-finders'. Around the cornice of the chapel runs a mosaic inscription on a gold ground, adapted from the passage in John 21 when Christ asks Peter three times if he loves him and Peter replies, 'Lord, thou knowest all things; thou knowest that I love thee.'

Relics of St John Chrysostom were preserved in an ancient granite basin in the Cappella del Coro **(13)**. The great preacher and Bishop of Constantinople died in 407. His relics were seized during the Fourth Crusade and brought from Constantinople to Rome. In 2004, eight hundred years after their looting, they were returned to the Ecumenical Patriarchate in Istanbul by Pope John Paul II.

The basilica has two prominent monuments to monarchs from Protestant countries who either renounced their thrones for the sake of their Catholic faith or were debarred from the succession because of it. Queen Christina of Sweden **(14)** abdicated when she became a Catholic and spent the rest of her life in Rome, dying here in 1689. James Stuart **(15)**, the would-be James III of England (he was recognised as such by France, Spain and Rome), died in Rome in 1766. His cenotaph by Canova, in the form of a sepulchral pyramid, commemorates him along with his sons, Henry and Charles Edward, 'Bonnie Prince Charlie'. Their tombs are in the crypt below.

Pope Benedict XVI appears at his window to bless the crowd and recite the *Angelus* with them.

The treasury **(16)** is entered from the north aisle. It contains many ecclesiastical treasures, some of them from the old basilica, and a particularly fine early Christian sarcophagus of the mid-fourth century. The vestments in which the bronze statue of St Peter is dressed on the day of his feast are also kept here.

The blessing on Sunday at noon

On your arrival in St Peter's Square you will see a great crowd assembled within the embrace of Bernini's colonnade, all with their eyes turned towards the Vatican Palace and the papal apartments. A crimson carpet indicates the window at which the pope will appear. Around the square are large screens showing the text of the *Angelus*, so that everyone can join in at the appropriate moment. The prayer goes as follows, interspersed with lines from the *Ave Maria* (for the text of the *Ave Maria*, see p. 275):

Angelus domini nuntiavit Mariae, et concepit de Spiritu Sancto. (Ave Maria...)	The Angel of the Lord declared unto Mary, and she conceived of the Holy Ghost.
Ecce ancilla Domini. Fiat mihi secundum verbum Tuum. (Ave maria...)	Behold the handmaid of the Lord. Be it unto me according to Thy word.
Et Verbum caro factum est et habitavit in nobis. (Ave Maria...)	And the Word was made flesh and dwelt among us.
Ora pro nobis Sancta Dei Genetrix,	Pray for us Holy Mother of God,
Ut dirigi efficiamur promissionibus Christi.	That we be made worthy of the promises of Christ.

The pope then addresses the crowd in a variety of languages, including Italian, English, German, French, Spanish, Polish and Czech.

SANTA MARIA MAGGIORE

Map p. 303, E2. Open 7–7.

The papal basilica of Santa Maria Maggiore stands on the Cispian summit of the Esquiline Hill. Its apse faces an obelisk, whose surface is devoid of inscription. Standing with your back to it and the basilica, and looking straight ahead down Via Depretis, which curves over two low ridges, you can see another distant obelisk at the top of the Spanish Steps and appreciate something of the plan of grand vistas that Pope Sixtus V, who lies buried here, designed for the city.

An interesting foundation legend attaches to Santa Maria Maggiore: the Virgin is said to have appeared to Pope Liberius on a hot August night in 358, telling him that in the morning he would find a patch of snow on the Esquiline Hill and that upon that patch of snow he should build a church. Liberius duly did so, and the building was known as the Liberian Basilica. When he died, two claimants emerged for the papal throne, Damasus (*see p. 183*) and Ursinus. Ursinus' faction barricaded themselves into the basilica whereupon Damasus authorised his men to remove part of the roof and pelt his rivals with missiles. Over a hundred died, but Damasus won the day. After 431, the year that the Council of Ephesus declared Mary to be the Mother of God, a new basilica was built and dedicated to the Virgin. That fifth-century foundation forms the nucleus of today's Santa Maria Maggiore.

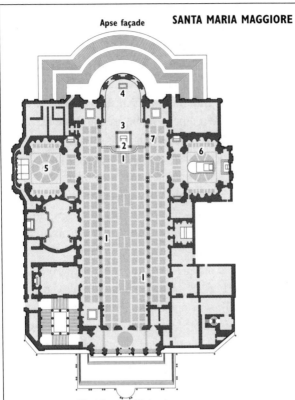

Apse façade **SANTA MARIA MAGGIORE**

West façade with loggia

1 **Fifth-century mosaics (above nave colonnade and on triumphal arch)**
2 **Confessio (relic of the Crib of Jesus)**
3 **High altar (relics of St Matthias)**
4 **Apse**
5 **Funeral chapel of Pope Paul V**
6 **Funeral chapel of Pope Sixtus V**
7 **Tomb-slab of Bernini**

HOLY DOORS

All four papal basilicas in Rome (St Peter's, Santa Maria Maggiore, San Paolo fuori le Mura and St John Lateran) have a *Porta Santa*, a Holy Door, usually the furthest right of the five entrances on the main west front (Santa Maria Maggiore is an exception, having its Holy Door on the left). This door is kept closed except in Holy Years, which occur every quarter of a century and when pilgrims to Rome are granted special indulgences. Other commemorative years are sometimes declared, and the Holy Doors thrown open, as they were for example during the Pauline Year of 2008, which celebrated two thousand years since the birth of St Paul. In this case the *Porta Santa* of San Paolo fuori le Mura was opened.

In preparation for a Holy Year, at St Peter's, it is the pope himself who opens the *Porta Santa*, on 24th December of the preceding year. At the other basilicas, the Holy Doors are opened by cardinals specially deputed to do so. The ceremony involves removing the temporary wall which blocks the door from the inside. In Santa Maria Maggiore, for example, you can see how impressively blocked the *Porta Santa* is, with a plaster casing. Once opened, the Holy Door remains so for twelve months. Its opening is a symbolic enactment by St Peter's successor of the unlocking of the Gates of Heaven by St Peter himself.

The Holy Door of Santa Maria Maggiore. The hands of Christ and the Virgin have been worn to shininess by the clasps of the faithful. The features of Christ seem to have been modelled on the imprint on the Turin Shroud. The Latin inscription at the top, 'Mother of God, Mother of the Church', refers to the declaration at the Council of Ephesus in 431 that Mary was the mother not only of a human son but of God. The present basilica of Santa Maria Maggiore was built soon after this declaration and dedicated to the Virgin.

The interior

The interior of the basilica is spacious and wide. Above the nave colonnades and on the triumphal arch **(1)** is a celebrated series of fifth-century mosaic panels, very difficult to see and appreciate, showing scenes from the Old Testament and of the life of Christ. In the confessio under the high altar **(2)**, in a silver and gilt tabernacle crowned by a figure of the Holy Child lying on a bed of straw, is preserved a piece of wood venerated as a fragment of the crib of the infant Jesus. In front of the altar, a larger-than-lifesize statue of Pope Pius IX kneels in adoration.

The high altar itself **(3)**, which rises above the confessio, is surmounted by a baldachin borne by four porphyry columns with gilded martyrs' palms wrapped around them. The altar contains the relics of St Matthias, the apostle who was chosen by lot to make up the Twelve after the exclusion of Judas (*Acts 1:26*). The baldachin is vast and tall, which makes it difficult to see and appreciate the apse mosaic (thirteenth century) **(4)** of the Coronation and Dormition of the Virgin. She sits enthroned with Christ, with a huge, twisting Tree of Life on either side.

Opening off each aisle is a large and sumptuous funeral chapel, the one on the left for Pope Paul V (Cappella Paolina) **(5)** and that on the right for Sixtus V **(6)**. Pope Pius V is also buried in the Cappella Paolina. Canonised in 1712, he was one of the great popes of the Counter-Reformation, committed to halting the spread of Protestantism and the spread of Islam. It was during his pontificate that the Christian fleet won its resounding victory over the Ottoman Turks at Lepanto. On the civic side, all three of these popes performed a valuable public service in reconstructing Rome's ancient aqueducts, restoring the supply of fresh water that had been so abundant in ancient times. Above the altar in the Cappella Paolina is a venerated icon of the Virgin and Child, the *Salus Populus Romani*, 'Salvation of the Roman People'. Until the thirteenth century, on 14th August, the eve of the feast of the Assumption, the icon of Christ from the Lateran (*see p. 69*) would be brought to Santa Maria Maggiore, where the Marian image was waiting on the front steps: thus Mary would greet her son. Legend attributes both icons to the hand of St Luke. Above the icon is a relief of Pope Liberius tracing the outline of his future basilica in a thick blanket of snow.

In humble contrast to these sumptuous funeral chapels, to the right of the sanctuary steps **(7)** is the simple tombslab of an architect who did much to glorify the papacy both in life and death: Gian Lorenzo Bernini (d. 1680).

The loggia on the west façade

Usually open at 9.30 and 1. Further information from the souvenir shop inside the basilica.

The main entrance front of Santa Maria Maggiore dates from 1743. Behind it and obscured by it, lies a late thirteenth-century façade, complete with mosaics. These include a depiction of Christ Pantocrator and four scenes below it showing the foundation legend of the basilica.

THE SEVEN PILGRIMAGE CHURCHES

A plan of Roman pilgrimage that included visits to the 'seven churches' was promoted by St Philip Neri in the sixteenth century. The churches in question were the four papal basilicas of St Peter's, St John Lateran, Santa Maria Maggiore and San Paolo fuori le Mura (*all described in previous chapters of this book*) together with the three minor basilicas of Santa Croce in Gerusalemme, San Lorenzo fuori le Mura and San Sebastiano (*described below*). San Sebastiano stands at the corner of the Via Appia and the Via delle Sette Chiese, the 'Road of the Seven Churches', the old pilgrims' route.

For the Holy Year of 2000, Pope John Paul II substituted another church for the basilica of San Sebastiano, the Santuario del Divino Amore in the southeastern suburbs. A shrine was first built on the site in 1740, at the place where a pilgrim had appealed (successfully) to a roadside image of the Madonna to protect him from ravening farm dogs. The modern sanctuary is easily accessible by bus 218, which leaves from Via Aradam just outside St John Lateran (*map p. 303, F4*). Night pilgrimages on foot set off for the sanctuary at midnight every Saturday from the first Saturday after Easter to the last Saturday in October, as well as on the night of 7th December, the eve of the Feast of the Immaculate Conception. Pilgrims meet at Piazza di Porta Capena (*map p. 303, D4*). The walk takes about five hours.

SANTA CROCE IN GERUSALEMME

Map p. 9. Open 7–12.45 & 3.30–7.30.

The basilica dedicated to the Holy Cross in Jerusalem stands on the site of a palace that once belonged to the mother of Constantine, St Helen, who claimed to have discovered the True Cross in Jerusalem. The present façade and much of the interior date from the eighteenth century, but the foundation is Helen's own, within the precincts of her palace, expressly to enshrine the fragment of the Cross that she brought back with her.

To get to the oldest part of the basilica, you go down a stepped ramp at the end of the south aisle. This takes you to the **Chapel of St Helen**, with a large statue of the saint holding a wooden Cross and two sculpted stone nails. Her clothing is surprisingly figure-hugging; she is remodelled from a Roman Juno. At the statue's foot, beneath a glass panel, on a place where soil from the Holy Land is said to have been deposited, are prayers inscribed on little slips of paper. The ceiling mosaic, originally made in the late fifteenth century, shows Christ and the Evangelists with Sts Peter and Paul as well as St Helen and St Sylvester, the pope who, according to a fictional medieval tradition, baptised Constantine. The last figure is the Spanish cardinal whose titular church this was when the mosaic was commissioned. St Helen died in 330 at a ripe old age. She was buried in a circular mausoleum on Via Labicana (Via Casilina), now ruined and not generally open to the public, though her splendid porphyry sarcophagus survives, in the Vatican Museums (*see p. 246*).

At the end of the north aisle is the entrance to the **Chapel of the Relics**, which contains items said to have been salvaged from the Holy Land by St Helen. These include the *Titulus Crucis*, the signboard inscribed INRI (*Iesus Nazarenus Rex Iudaeorum*; 'Jesus of Nazareth, King of the Jews'), which was found behind a wall here in the fifteenth century during building work. Pope Alexander VI (the notorious Rodrigo Borgia) immediately authenticated the discovery and sent out a bull, *Admirabile sacramentum*, conferring a plenary indulgence on all those who visited the basilica on the last Sunday in January.

The approach to the relics is solemn, along a corridor clad in travertine and unpolished green-grey marble, designed in 1930 by the Fascist-era architect Florestano di Fausto. The whole place has a deeply penitential atmosphere, made more brooding still if you first visit the chapel of Antonietta Meo, 'Nannolina', who died of bone cancer at the age of six, having lost a leg to the disease if we can believe the mural decoration, and in her pain and existential bewilderment having written over a hundred letters to God, Christ and the Virgin.

You ascend to the Chapel of the Relics by a series of stepped platforms flanked by bronze Stations of the Cross between which are placed Latin texts from the liturgy of Good Friday, forming a path of meditation. The final text, on the left, announces: 'Behold the wood of the Cross, to which the Saviour of the world was pinned. O come let us adore.' You now enter the vestibule to the chapel proper, decorated with inlaid marble wall panels of tall, slender candlesticks, with a single, ivory-coloured, static-flamed taper standing in each. On the wall to your right is the brick behind which the Titulus was found.

The relics, kept in six precious reliquaries, are as follows: fragments of the True Cross; the Titulus; one of the nails with which Christ was fixed to the Cross; two thorns from his crown; a finger bone of St Thomas (perhaps the very one which felt Christ's wounds?); and part of the Cross of the good thief. The fragments of the Cross, Titulus and nail are the relics said to have been brought here by St Helen. The Crown of Thorns was looted from Constantinople during the Fourth Crusade by the Venetians, through whom it passed to France, where it remains to this day, preserved in the Sainte-Chapelle. It is completely devoid of thorns, all of them having been dispersed to churches around the globe. Whether all those relics claimed as holy thorns once sprang from the same plant is not for this book to say. It for each of us to decide, when looking upon these things, how authentic we believe them to be, or even how authentic we need them to be, in order to believe that two thousand years ago, on a hill called Golgotha, in Jerusalem, under the rule of the emperor Tiberius and the governorship of Pontius Pilate, a man called Jesus was crucified for his unorthodox convictions and thereby saved mankind.

CRUCIFIXION

Let this mind be in you, which was also in Christ Jesus: who, being in the form of God, thought it not robbery to be equal with God, but made himself of no reputation, and took upon him the form of a servant, and was made in the likeness of men. And being found in fashion as a man, he humbled himself, and became obedient unto death, even the death of the cross. Wherefore God also hath highly exalted him, and given him a name which is above every name, that at the name of Jesus every knee should bow, of things in heaven, and things in earth, and things under the earth; and that every tongue should confess that Jesus Christ is Lord, to the glory of God the Father.

Philippians 2:5–11

Of all the many ways there are to die, crucifixion is one of the worst. As a form of execution it was in use for about a thousand years, from the sixth century BC. A crucified person could take several days to die. Exhaustion from the perpetual effort of keeping one's body raised so as not to crush the lungs could eventually lead to collapse and asphyxiation. Otherwise, death might result from blood poisoning or from dehydration. Bodily functions—urination and defecation—obviously had to be performed on the cross, which would attract flies and derision. There was nothing a victim could do against the itching and discomfort. The pain, also, was intense and grew worse as the days wore on. The Romans reserved this particular form of cruelty for the lowest of all criminals: slaves or traitors to the state. To be crucified was the greatest of all humiliations. It is no coincidence that God's own son, who had first so humbled himself as to be born of a human woman, was done to death in this way, the meanest of all ways. The tree of shame became for Christians the tree of glory.

Constantine abolished crucifixion in 337, the year of his conversion as well as of his death. As a means of execution it was replaced with the *furca*, an early form of gallows.

The Alexamenos graffito, found on the Palatine Hill and now on display in the Palatine Museum, is a second-century piece of graffiti deriding Christians for their worship of a common criminal, a man so low that he was condemned to die on a cross. He is shown with the head of a donkey. The Greek inscription reads: 'Alexamenos worships his god'.

SAN LORENZO FUORI LE MURA

Map p. 9. Open 8–12 & 4–6.30. It is best to visit in the after-noon since funerals are often held in the morning. Bus 71 from Piazza San Silvestro (map p. 302, C1), tram 19 from Piazza Risorgimento (Vatican), bus 3 from the Colosseum.

The basilica of San Lorenzo stands in unattractive sur-roundings on a busy road opposite a bus terminus. Let this not put you off. Its atmosphere of peaceful spiritual-ity makes it one of the loveliest early Christian basilicas in the city and it is well worth the journey to get here.

The basilica is dedicated to St Lawrence, thought to have been a deacon of the early Church. Despite the tradition that he was roasted alive on a gridiron, he was probably in fact beheaded in 258 during the persecutions of Valerian, in the same year that the bodies of St Peter and St Paul may have been moved to the catacombs of St Sebastian for temporary safekeeping. Lawrence was bur-ied here, in the cemetery known as the Campo Verano (after the second-century emperor Lucius Verus, whose land this had been) and his cult was established in the city soon afterwards. By the fourth century he was con-sidered one of the patron saints of Rome, together with St Peter and St Paul. Campo Verano is still a cemetery; its cy-press trees rise dark and tall behind the basilica building.

San Lorenzo is a Constantinian foundation, rebuilt and radically altered over the years, most notably in 1216, when its orientation was changed, placing the entrance at the opposite end from previously (this explains why today the triumphal arch, with its exquisite mosaic, faces away from the congregation).

The exterior entrance porch is a reconstruction of the thirteenth-century original. It is supported by six Ionic columns, four of which are fluted. Above the architrave is a pretty Cosmatesque frieze with a little Agnus Dei in a roundel. Under the porch are three ancient sarcophagi and frescoes of the lives of the two deacon-saints, Lawrence and Stephen.

The interior has a lovely Cosmatesque floor, predominantly purple and green, and a Cosmatesque pulpit. In the confessio beneath the fine twelfth-century baldachin are the relics of St Lawrence and two companions, Stephen and Justin. Beyond this is the chancel, raised above the level of the main church. On the triumphal arch is a sixth-century mosaic of Christ seated on a globe flanked by St Peter, St Paul, St Stephen, St Lawrence, St Hippolytus and Pope Pelagius II offering a model of the church. Beneath the two latticed windows are representations of Bethlehem and Jerusalem, respectively the scenes of Christ's birth and death.

Under the chancel, where the marble slab on which St Lawrence's body was placed after his martyrdom is also displayed, is the mausoleum of Pius IX (*see box on p. 103*). The pontiff lies in a crystal casket, his face hidden under a silver mask. His body qualifies as incorrupt.

INCORRUPTIBILITY

All flesh is grass, and all the goodliness thereof is as the flower of the field: The grass withereth, the flower fadeth: because the spirit of the Lord bloweth upon it: surely the people is grass. The grass withereth, the flower fadeth: but the word of our God shall stand for ever.

Isaiah 40:6–8

But some people's flesh, it seems, is not grass. Their mortal remains do not decay but are preserved incorrupt down the generations for all to marvel at as a token of the immortality which is the hope of us all. The Apostles' Creed contains the line 'we look for the resurrection of the body' (*carnis resurrectionem*). It is very clear: the flesh will rise again. The Nicene Creed puts it differently, trusting instead in the 'resurrection of the dead' (*resurrectionem mortuorum*). The distinction is not altogether trivial. Does resurrection have to be corporeal? Christ, after all, was resurrected in body. The stone was found rolled away and his corpse was nowhere to be seen. But who else can expect to be so raised? People worried about this greatly in the Middle Ages. Some contended that fleshly resurrection would clothe us in a better body than before: not only would physical disabilities disappear, but women would even be able to enter heaven as men.

Others fretted that resurrection would not be able to take place if a person's body was not intact.

Today, all over the Roman Catholic world, the bodies of saints that have not putrefied as other bodies do are exposed to the wondering gaze of all comers, as a symbol of hope in the life to come.

The cloister

The cloister, surrounding a little garden, has fragments of pagan and Early Christian inscriptions on its walls. A shell from 1943 is kept here, a relic of the Allied attack that struck San Lorenzo instead of its intended target, Tiburtina railway station. The Catacombs of St Cyriaca are entered from here (on request). It is here that the body of St Lawrence is said to have been placed after his martyrdom. Cyriaca was a Roman woman who gave sanctuary to St Lawrence and eventually suffered martyrdom herself. Many of the inscriptions on the cloister walls are from these catacombs.

SAN SEBASTIANO

Map p. 9. Open 8.30–12 & 2–5. Closed Sun.
The first basilica of San Sebastiano was built in the fourth century by Pope Damasus I (*see p. 183*) over the cata-

combs where the martyred St Sebastian was buried and where, according to tradition, the bodies of St Peter and St Paul had been temporarily moved to safeguard them from desecration during the persecutions of Valerian in the mid-third century. The present church, with its graceful portico, is an early seventeenth-century rebuilding. It can be visited for itself, or as part of a guided tour of the Catacombs of San Sebastiano (*see p. 27*).

On the north side is the Chapel of St Sebastian, which houses the saint's relics as well as a statue showing him wounded and swooning, designed by Bernini and executed by his follower Antonio Giorgetti. Very little is known about Sebastian, beyond the fact of his martyrdom sometime in the third century. The manner of his death is disputed. Popular tradition clings to the story that he was pierced to death by arrows, an idea that has appealed to painters and sculptors. In the opposite chapel, the Chapel of the Relics, an arrow is displayed in a reliquary casket, along with the original stone from Domine Quo Vadis, said to preserve the imprint of Christ's feet (*see p. 26*).

The painted wooden ceiling of the basilica is especially beautiful. In the four outer corners is the black Borghese eagle, a reference to Cardinal Scipione Borghese, nephew of Pope Paul V, for whom this basilica was reconstructed. In the centre is a scene of St Sebastian bound to a tree trunk, with a Roman soldier behind him with a quiver full of arrows and an angel above, bringing down a golden crown from heaven. At the corners are palms of martyrdom and on either side are palms and an arrow within an encircling crown. It is the work of the Dutch-born master Jan van Santen (Giovanni Vasanzio), who was a favourite architect of the Borghese family.

POPE PIUS IX

For many people, Pius IX, Giovanni Maria Mastai-Ferretti, the longest-serving of all the popes (1846–78), is also one of the greatest. His ecclesiastical impact was considerable: he defined the doctrine of the Immaculate Conception of the Blessed Virgin in 1854, declaring her free from original sin; and the doctrine of papal infallibility in 1870. Politically he was unequal to the demands placed upon him. Though he began his reign on a tide of popularity, greeted with enthusiasm by the intelligentsia, who saw him as a liberal and a reformer, he had not the slightest intention of renouncing papal sovereignty. Italy was in a ferment, and one by one the lands of St Peter either ceded themselves to the nationalists or were conquered by them. Pope Pius retreated behind a reactionary wall. Garibaldi had no respect for him and named his horse after him as a signal of his contempt. In 1870 Rome finally fell to the Italian armies and papal rule in Italy came to an end. Pope Pius retired to Vatican, where he died eight years later.

His legacy today is mixed. He had many detractors in his lifetime: his funeral cortège was intercepted on its way to San Lorenzo fuori le Mura by a band of anti-clerical protesters who attempted to tip his coffin into the Tiber. Those protesters are still vocal: you don't have to look very hard on the Internet before you see Pope Pius arraigned as one of the most evil people of his age, accused of all manner of diabolical activity including aiding and abetting the slave trade, making conditions ripe for civil war in America and establishing the Sicilian Mafia. He was beatified by Pope John Paul II in 2000. At his mausoleum under San Lorenzo fuori le Mura, prayer cards for his glorification have been placed on the rail by the Pius IX Museum in Senigallia, the town of his birth near Ancona. Upon them, in his own handwriting, is reproduced the following Latin prayer: *Accelera Domine ut eruas nos*, O Lord make haste to deliver us.

Though of little use against political and ecclesiastical rivals on a world stage where history-shaping events were being acted out, Pius seems to have been a 'nice person'. He was also, if we can believe a *New York Times* correspondent of 1867, blessed with good looks, having the 'pleasantest face I have seen in Europe.' Excelsis Fine Fragrances of San Rafael, California, have created an 'aristocratic, old-world aftershave' dubbed The Pope's Cologne, inspired by this controversial man.

AD CATACUMBAS
THE CATACOMBS

The ancient Romans originally cremated their dead and buried them outside the city, by the edges of busy roads, where relatives could easily come and make libations at the tomb. The early Christians, in common with the Jews from whom their tradition derived, inhumed the deceased. The very earliest burials, such as that of St Peter himself, took place alongside pagan graves, in burial grounds common to all. As space began to grow short, Christians went further afield, and naturally enough they chose to be laid to rest *apud sanctos*, 'among the saints', in other words alongside the martyrs who had been buried out beside the consular roads. The land that borders many of those roads is riddled with tombs. In many cases the ground had already been dug by quarrymen and the soft volcanic tufa of the disused shafts was easy to work. The ground around the Via Appia, the Via Nomentana and the Via Salaria is undermined now by many miles of tunnels, most of them stacked layer on layer.

Contrary to popular legend, the catacombs were never secret, nor were they used as hiding places. It is true that Christians were members of a minority sect, until the mid-fourth century often persecuted, but their choice to go underground was not the result of any need to be hidden. Rome's earliest Christians were converted Jews. The Jews were never persecuted, but their dead also lie buried in very similar arrangements of subterranean, rock-hewn graves. The Christians simply continued this tradition.

The Christian catacombs were not originally used as places of cult. The earliest communities met in the houses of their wealthier co-religionists (*see p. 122*). Groups of mourners would come to the catacombs to hold commemorative feasts on the anniversaries of martyrs' deaths or of the deaths of members of their families. However, by the late fourth century, altars were being set up in the catacombs, for example by Pope Damasus in the Catacombs of San Callisto, and today it is possible (by prior arrangement) to celebrate Mass in them.

After Christianity became the official religion of the Empire, many of the more prominent catacomb burials were reinterred in the city: it is said that twenty-eight cartloads of martyrs' bones were brought to the Pantheon alone, the great circular pagan temple which was consecrated under the name of Santa Maria ad Martyres. Little by little the catacombs, the underground cities of the dead, were forgotten. From the sixteenth century they began to be rediscovered, and since then they have been an important stage on all pilgrims' routes in Rome.

Features of the catacombs

There are many catacombs underneath the soil of suburban Rome, and though all of them are different, they all also share a number of common features. Typically, they are named after a prominent saint who was buried there (San Sebastiano, Sant'Agnese) or else they take their name from the person who gave a grant of land for their construction (Priscilla, Domitilla). The approach to them is down a narrow flight of steps, often leading from a church that had latterly been erected over the site. The grave types take various forms:

Loculi: shelves cut in the rock into which the body was placed, strewn with quicklime and wrapped in a winding sheet. The loculus was then closed up with a marble or terracotta slab;

Arcosolia: arched recesses let into the wall. The back wall of the recess is typically inscribed with the family's name and is sometimes adorned with wall-paintings. Sometimes the recess contains a tomb-chest or an altar.

Chapels: self-contained rooms, sometimes quite spacious, with several tombs, typically belonging to a single family or containing important burials. There are often low stone benches around the walls, for use during commemorative banquets.

Common to all the catacombs is the sense they give of the humility, unity and profound faith of the early Roman Christians. On a visit to any of them, even to the most

Examples of Christian symbols commonly found in the catacombs:

1) Chi Rho, the superimposed letters X and P, the first two letters of the Greek word ΧΡΙΣΤΟΣ (Christ);

2) Chi Rho with the Alpha and Omega (A and Ω; also written ω), the first and last letters of the Greek alphabet, signifying the beginning and the end. 'I am Alpha and Omega, the beginning and the ending, saith the Lord, which was, and which is to come.' *Revelation 1:8*;

3) The anchor, symbol of hope, specifically of the hope of resurrection;

4) The dove and olive branch. The dove is a symbol of the Holy Spirit and a reference to the dove that appeared to Noah to signal the end of the Flood and of God's wrath. In a funerary context, the symbolism is of the repose of the soul of the deceased in the peace of Christ;

5) Praying figure. Early Christian representations of prayer show the faithful raising his or her hands to Heaven, in the posture known as 'orans', mimicking Christ's arms stretched upon the Cross;

6) Palm branch and stylised ivy leaf. The palm is a symbol of the Tree of Life and of victory over death. Evergreen ivy stands for everlasting life.

primitive, you have a strong impression of the solidarity of this early community, when threats of violence and death came from without, before Christianity became the sole faith and internal dissent brought threats of violence and death from within.

Inscriptions in the catacombs

Burials in the catacombs were identified in a variety of ways. Because many of the people buried here were illiterate, the graves are often marked by niches scooped out of the wall into which identifying tokens would have been placed, or by a scratched Christian symbol or a symbol of the trade of the deceased. Written inscriptions are either in Greek (the earlier burials) or Latin. Greek inscriptions typically begin with some kind of variation on the words ΕΝΘΑΔΕ ΚΕΙΤΑΙ, 'Here lies...', followed by the name. In Latin inscriptions, the name of a whole family is often given (eg: '*Locus Africani et Rufini*', the plot of the Africani and Rufini). When individuals are commemorated, the number of years, months and days they lived is often noted—a feature also of pagan Roman tombstones.

VISITING THE CATACOMBS

All the catacombs are visited by guided tour only. For the less-frequented catacombs you will need to book in advance. For popular ones such as San Sebastiano, you can often just turn

up. See the entries below for opening times and contact details.
Catacomb tours typically last about half an hour. NB: Open-
ing times are always subject to change: check before you visit.
It is possible to arrange to celebrate Mass in the catacombs; in
each case, contact the catacomb directly.

CATACOMBS ON & AROUND THE VIA APPIA

Catacombs of San Sebastiano
Map p. 9. Open 9–12 & 2–5. Closed Sun.
These are some of the best-known of all the Roman catacombs, combining many interesting features and famed
for their association with St Peter and St Paul. The catacombs themselves are described on p. 27 and the basilica
church above them on p. 101.

Catacombs of Domitilla
Map p. 9. Open 9–12 & 2–5. T: 06 511 0342, www.dom-
itilla.info. Closed Tues and in Jan. Entrance on Via delle Sette
Chiese.
These very extensive catacombs (about 15km of tunnels)
occupy land that belonged to Flavia Domitilla, a patrician lady of the family of the emperor Domitian who was
exiled for her Christian faith. The catacombs were in use
from the first century AD, making this one of the oldest
Christian burial grounds in the world. The early martyrs
Nereus and Achilleus were buried here, until the translation of their relics to the church that bears their name

'Flavia Faustina, lived two years, eight months and eight days.' Her father was presumably a cooper.

near the Baths of Caracalla (*see p. 23*). An inscription by Pope Damasus honours the saints as soldiers of the imperial army, who obeyed orders to execute Christians until suddenly they saw the error of their ways, whereupon they cast away their swords and shields and submitted to a martyr's death. Their semi-underground basilica was an important medieval pilgrimage destination. The catacombs contain fine wall-paintings, including a second-century *Good Shepherd*, the earliest such representation known in a Christian context.

Catacombs of San Callisto

Map p. 9. Open 9–12 & 2–5. Closed Wed and in Feb. T: 06 513 0151, www.catacombe.roma.it. Entrance on the peaceful road between the Via Appia and Via Ardeatina.

These catacombs were the first official burial place of the popes, many of whom died martyr's deaths. St Cecilia was laid to rest here after her martyrdom in 230 (her body was later moved to the church in Trastevere that bears her name; *see p. 144*). St Tarcisius, patron saint of altar servers, was also interred here after being killed by a mob to whom he refused to deliver up the Blessed Sacrament. Tarcisius' relics were later moved to the church of San Silvestro in Capite (*see p. 195*), at a time when the relics of many martyrs were being moved from the catacombs to places of worship within the city.

The Catacombs of San Callisto take their name from Calixtus, an early third-century deacon to whose care this burial ground was entrusted by Pope Zephyrinus. The guided tour takes in the so-called Crypt of the Popes, with the tomb-niches of nine martyred pontiffs of the third century: Pontianus, Anterus, Fabian, Lucius I, Stephen I, Sixtus II, Dionysius I, Felix I and Eutychianus. Fragments of some of their tomb-slabs remain, as well as a verse inscription by Pope Damasus I (*see p. 183*) honouring Pope Sixtus by name. Also shown on the tour are the original resting place of St Cecilia and a chapel with fine wall-paintings.

The **Catacombs of Praetextatus**, site of the capture and subsequent beheading of Pope Sixtus II in 258, during the persecutions of Valerian (when St Lawrence was also martyred), are not regularly open to the public.

CATACOMBS ON VIA NOMENTANA & VIA SALARIA

Catacombs of Sant'Agnese

Map p. 9. Via Nomentana 349. Bus 60 from Piazza Venezia and Via Nazionale to the XXI Aprile stop. Open Tues–Sat 9–12 & 4–6. It is best to book a tour in advance: T: 06 861 0840, catacombe@santagnese.it.

For a description of the basilica of Sant'Agnese, see p. 162. The catacombs are entered from the basilica narthex. The catacombs were in use from the third to the fourth centuries. There are no wall-paintings here, but plenty of interesting inscriptions. The body of St Agnes was placed in a silver coffer donated by Pope Paul V in 1615. It still contains her relics except for the head, which is in the church of Sant'Agnese in Agone on Piazza Navona.

Catacombs of Priscilla

Map p. 9. Open Tues–Sun 8.30–12 & 2.30–4; closed Mon and in Jan; T: 06 8620 6272. You should ring ahead to book a time and specify the language you need. Entrance at no. 430 Via Salaria. Bus 92 from Termini Station or 63 from Piazza Venezia (nearest stop, Via di Priscilla).

These are extremely extensive catacombs (about 13km), and very rewarding to visit. They occupy land donated by Priscilla, a wealthy patrician. Two popes of the early fourth century, Marcellinus and Marcellus I, were buried here, and a number of later popes, including Sylvester I and Liberius, were buried in the vicinity. The site is now occupied by a Benedictine convent.

The catacombs contain many interesting second-to-third-century wall-paintings, including the oldest-known representation of the Madonna and Child; a *Good Shepherd*; *Daniel in the Lion's Den* and the *Sacrifice of Isaac*. The *Velata* is a tripartite scene of a woman (presumably the deceased) shown in an attitude of prayer between scenes of her marriage and motherhood. Especially fine is the Greek Chapel, known from its Greek dedication from a certain Obrimos, 'in loving memory of my sweet wife Nestoriana'. Its decoration includes a scene of the breaking of bread.

THE EUCHARIST

The feast of the Eucharist, also known as Holy Communion, has its origins in the traditional Jewish passover meal which Christ ate with his disciples on the same night that he was betrayed. The term Eucharist, from the Greek word for thanksgiving, may refer to Christ's offering of thanks to God when he broke the bread or to a more general offer of thanksgiving by all Christians for the sacrifice which Christ made for mankind. The idea that Christ's divine presence inhabits the bread and the wine comes very clearly from Christ himself: 'Take, eat; this is my body... Drink ye all of it; for this is my blood.' (*Matthew 26.*)

The notion that this identification might be seen as something more than symbolic had a long gestation; and at the Fourth Lateran Council in 1215, Pope Innocent III promulgated the doctrine of transubstantiation. The outward appearance of the Host remains the same but in essence it is transformed into Christ's actual body and blood.

The way Communion is taken today, with the members of the congregation moving in single file to the altar to receive it, was unknown in early Christian communities. Instead, the Eucharist was celebrated as a communal meal, as described in Acts 2:42 where new converts 'continued steadfastly in the apostles' doctrine and fellowship, and in breaking of bread, and in prayers.' A late second-century wall-painting in the Catacombs of Priscilla shows just such a scene, with a group of celebrants gathered around a table to break bread together.

THE AVENTINE, CAELIAN & TRASTEVERE

ON THE TRAIL OF THE EARLY CHRISTIANS

On a warm February morning, a man sits in the sun on the steps that lead up to the church of Santa Prisca, sifting through the thick wad of old bus tickets and receipts that have accumulated in his wallet. Young American students walk by in twos, chatting loudly as they go: 'I'm like, come on, there's no freaking way I would *do* that!' Green parakeets shriek garrulously in the Giardino degli Aranci, a pleasant, sequestered spot with benches and orange trees and gravel walks, and stunning views across the city. On the entrance door of the next-door basilica of Santa Sabina, a notice is pinned up announcing that on the coming Ash Wednesday, His Holiness the Pope will celebrate Mass with the imposition of ashes. This is the Aventine Hill, home to three ancient *tituli*: Santa Sabina, Santa Prisca and Santa Balbina. It is a quiet area of red-plastered villas and small apartment blocks, secluded behind garden walls and shaded by umbrella pines. Its sights can comfortably be fitted into a morning or an afternoon.

Santa Sabina
Map p. 301, A1. Open 6.30–12.45 & 3–7.
The basilica dedicated to St Sabina is one of the loveliest

and most atmospheric in Rome. It is named in honour of an early second-century Roman matron, who according to legend was converted to Christianity by her slave Serapia and was martyred for her faith around 126. Her relics were brought here and a church was erected over the spot in the fifth century. In the early thirteenth century Pope Honorius III donated it to St Dominic, for the use of his Order. The adjoining convent still preserves the room where St Dominic lived.

The basilica has a particularly fine west door, made of carved cypress wood. It dates from the early fifth century, which makes it contemporary with the church's foundation. It is formed of twenty-eight panels (ten of which—the ones at easy removal level—have been lost) showing Old and New Testament scenes with a famous representation of the Crucifixion in the top left-hand corner. This is the earliest known depiction of the Crucifixion in Western art[9], and the Cross itself is merely hinted at, perhaps revealing the terrible stigma that attached to this form of execution, which in the Roman world was a mark of extreme shame, reserved for the lowest of all criminals. To depict God meeting death in such a way was something that early artists may have shrunk from doing. The famous second-century Alexamenos graffito reveals the derision to which Christians were subject.

9   It might be safer to say in Western *public* art. There is a beautiful panel in the British Museum, part of an ivory casket, probably also made in Rome, and dated c. 420–30. It shows the Crucifixion and the suicide of Judas.

It shows a donkey upon a cross with a man saluting it and the scrawled sneer: 'Alexamenos worships his god' (*see illustration on p. 97*). Public shame can be a powerful deterrent, except to the very strong-minded. As St Paul remarks: 'We preach Christ crucified, unto the Jews a stumbling-block, and unto the Greeks foolishness; But unto them which are called, both Jews and Greeks, Christ the power of God, and the wisdom of God. Because the foolishness of God is wiser than men; and the weakness of God is stronger than men.' (*1 Corinthians 1:23–25*). In Rome, after his arrest, St Paul was deserted by many of his followers because they were ashamed of his chains.

Inside Santa Sabina, there is an atmosphere of calm stillness, an atmosphere of ages. The basilica is wide and spacious and beautiful, its grave and sober lines uncluttered by seating. The revetment of the apse is very simple: vertical strips of porphyry dividing marble panels sliced in half into thin sheets, folded out so their web of veining matches in perfect mirror symmetry. In the nave, a sheet of perspex has been placed over the pavement mosaic of the early Dominican friar Fra' Muñoz de Zamora. At the west end, a surviving section of mosaic from the original decoration shows two female figures representing the converted Jews ('*ex circumcisione*') and the converted Gentiles ('*ex gentibus*'). The stone screens in front of the schola cantorum (*example illustrated opposite*) are carved with a design of scrolled crosses, cypress trees and rosettes, a design that seems to belong to the iconoclastic period of the eighth

century, when all representation of the godhead was for-
bidden and only symbolic references were allowed. Christ
would not be shown as a man, for example, but his body
might be shown in the form of the Eucharistic bread. And
indeed we find that symbol here, all the way up the nave
in the spandrels of the colonnade, in the form of an inlaid
marble design of monstrances holding Communion wa-
fers. But before we get carried away, we should remember
that Byzantium failed utterly to impose iconoclasm upon
Rome, and that the 'antique' atmosphere of this church is
the result of a remodelling after 1936.

Sant'Alessio

Map p. 301, A1; open 8.30–12.30 & 3.30–5, sometimes 6.

Sant'Alessio is one of the churches that was visited by Sigeric (*see p. 148*), but nothing remains of it as it was in Sigeric's day. He would be interested to know, though, that the altar in the Romanesque crypt preserves relics of one of his successors, a later Archbishop of Canterbury, Thomas Becket, who held the position from 1162–70. Sadly the entrance to the crypt, to the left of the high altar, is usually padlocked, with an air of hopeless finality. The faithful sit instead in contemplation before a twelfth/thirteenth-century icon of the Virgin at the end of the south aisle, where a large sign announces that the chapel is alarmed. There is a fondness for signs at Sant'Alessio. Pinned to the entrance door, a note reminds all comers that a church is different from a street or a museum, a supermarket or office, or even from one's own home. One might begin to feel hectored did it not go on to say that it was a place reserved for 'personal silence'. In a world where we are all encouraged to be so public, this feels good.

At the west end of the church, looking like part of a stage set, is a wood and stucco ensemble showing St Alessio (Alexis) under the stairs of his house. According to his story, this saint, the son of a Roman senator, renounced his pagan beliefs on his wedding day and went out into the world as a mendicant. He later applied to his own family for a job as a servant, and died unrecognised by them under the stairs of his former home.

The view through the keyhole

Very close to Sant'Alessio, in Piazza dei Cavallieri di Malta, you will probably see a huddle of people eagerly taking turns to peer at a closed door. They have come to this otherwise little-frequented spot to view (and attempt to photograph) the dome of St Peter's, perfectly framed by an avenue of evergreens, as seen through the keyhole of the entrance portal of the Priorato di Malta, the residence of the ambassador of the Knights of Malta to Italy and the Holy See. The square is a wide open space, given a rather gross backdrop of obelisks and carved knightly insignia

The keyhole. The paint all around it has been worn away. This photograph is a failure. The aim is to not to take a snapshot of keyhole itself, however sharp and in focus, but of what you can see through it.

by Piranesi. The tall, dark pines of Sant'Anselmo rise behind. The keyhole phenomenon is quite popular. People
sometimes even arrive by car to view it. Having briefly
looked, they take their photograph and drive away again.
It has become a ritual. We are all peering through the
keyhole in search of some kind of metaphysical reward.

THE DOMUS ECCLESIA & THE TITULUS

The earliest Christian communities in Rome did not
have permanent churches dedicated solely to the purpose of worship. When St Paul writes, 'Greet Priscilla
and Aquila my helpers in Christ Jesus: Likewise greet
the church that is in their house' (*Romans 16:3,5*), he is
referring to a *domus ecclesiae*, that is a private house that
was used as a meeting place for members of the Christian community. The first permanent meeting halls in
Rome were known as *tituli*, presumably from the notice
or emblem that was hung up outside to identify them
(a *titulus* is literally a signboard). *Tituli* were typically
known also by the name of their founder, usually the
owner of the land on which they stood, thus *Titulus
Clementis*, 'at the sign of Clement', now the church of
San Clemente. San Lorenzo in Lucina was the *Titulus
Lucinae*, named after the Roman matron whose land it
occupied or whose house was made over to Christian
worship. By the end of the fifth century there were just
over two dozen such *tituli* in Rome. Some have been

discovered with bath houses attached, leading scholars to suppose that baptisms took place there. Although it is very tempting to identify the church of Santa Prisca as the very *Titulus Priscae* that St Paul would have known as Priscilla's *domus ecclesia*, the identification cannot be confirmed and thus is not accepted.

When we talk of titular churches today, we mean churches that are in the care of a cardinal-priest. All cardinals holding this rank are appointed to a church in Rome. At the time of writing, there were one hundred and forty-nine such cardinals in office.

Santa Prisca

Map p. 301, B1. Mithraeum open by appointment on the 2nd and 4th Sunday of the month at 4pm for individual visitors and at 3pm and 5pm for groups; T: 06 39967700.

The simple façade of Santa Prisca, in yellow brick, is articulated by a pedimented door, announcing, with admirable concision: 'S. Prisca'. The church probably doesn't stand on the site of the *domus ecclesia* of St Paul's friend Prisca, husband of Aquila the tent-maker, whom he salutes in his Epistle to the Romans. Nevertheless, it is an ancient foundation, and other mystery cults besides Christianity have found the soil congenial here. Under the church a Mithraeum has been discovered and a superb opus sectile head

of Sol that was excavated here (*illustrated left*) is now part of the Museo Nazionale display in Palazzo Massimo, near the Baths of Diocletian (*for more on the cult of Mithras, see p. 140*).

Santa Balbina

Map p. 301, B2.

The basilica of St Balbina, dedicated to the second-century virgin martyr of that name, stands on the lower slopes of the ancient *Aventinus Minor*, the Lesser Aventine, at the point where the hill curves down to the valley of the Circus Maximus. At the time of writing, the church was open only for half an hour each day (*12.30–1; 10.30–11 on Sun*). I went at four o'clock on a sunny afternoon, the hour when most Roman churches are throwing open their doors after the midday rest. But all was still at Santa Balbina. It was undergoing restoration and there was a notice pinned up on the gate saying that because of this they were unable to take wedding bookings. Stubbornness takes hold at moments like these, and inaccessible places assume the features of El Dorado. Santa Balbina's worn, caramel-coloured brick façade and its three wide-arched windows seemed to hold so much promise. The floor is said to be set with

fine mosaics, perhaps taken from the Baths of Caracalla, whose ruins this tantalising little church overlooks...

There is a bus stop nearby and a convenient fallen section of fluted column to sit on to wait, on a patch of grass beside the busy Via Baccelli. It can take as long as thirty-five minutes before a bus (no. 160) draws up to take you away. I did begin to wonder if I should give up the trip to Santa Balbina. Would anyone come to deal with that final-looking padlock at 12.30 the following day?

They did. As the appointed hour approached, a small congregation began to gather and a smiling priest arrived to celebrate Mass. And the mosaics turned out to be as fine as promised (*illustrations above*). Black and white, a mixture of figurative and geometric. One of them has symbols of the Zodiac, another a large water jar, and another a dove with sprigs of olive. They are not from the Baths of Caracalla but from a first-century necropolis. On

the south side is a much venerated fifteenth-century relief of the Crucifixion by Mino da Fiesole and Giovanni
Dalmata.

Santa Balbina was founded in the fifth century on the
site of the house of a Roman consul, Lucius Fabius Cilo.
The house had been a gift to Cilo from the emperor Caracalla, after the emperor had been embarrassed by his
henchmen's zealous attempt to dispose of Cilo during
the purges which accompanied Caracalla's murder of
his brother and co-ruler Geta. Their father, Septimius
Severus, had hoped that his two boys would rule jointly
and harmoniously. It was not to be. Caracalla disposed
of Geta and then subjected him to a *damnatio memoriae*,
expunging his image from official statuary and picking
the letters of his name off their triumphal arch in the Forum (the Arch of Septimius Severus). Caracalla's baths
were completed in 217, five years after his murder of his
brother. The ruins are impressive (*open 9–dusk; until 1pm
on Mon*) and are famed as the spot where Shelley wrote
his *Prometheus Unbound*.

THE CAELIAN HILL

The atmosphere of the Caelian Hill (Monte Celio) is very
different from the Aventine. In early times it was a residential area and the site of a large food market as well
as two barracks and the temple of the deified emperor

Claudius. During the time of St Peter and St Paul's ministry in Rome, this is the character it would have had. The Colosseum at its foot had yet to be built.

On the southwest flank of the hill is the church of St Gregory the Great (**San Gregorio Magno**; *map p. 303, D4*), popular for weddings (its wide steps are superb for photography). St Gregory founded a monastery here, on the site of his family home, and lived a monastic life within it until called to the papacy in 590. Though he had accepted the tiara only reluctantly, his reign was a brilliant one, establishing Roman authority in spiritual matters and in temporal afffairs laying the foundation for future papal power. It was from this monastery in 596 that St Augustine and his band of monks set out to evangelise the English.

Further up the hill is the church of **Santi Giovanni e Paolo**, also popular for weddings—so popular, in fact, that the urns for flowers which line the nave are never taken away. Underneath this church are some very interesting excavations, described below:

The excavations under Santi Giovanni e Paolo

Map p. 301, C1 or p. 303, E4. Open 10–1 & 3–6; closed Tues and Wed, www.caseromane.it.

Entered from the narrow Clivo di Scauro, underneath the church of Santi Giovanni e Paolo, are the excavated remains of ancient houses, a street and shops, dating

from the first to the fifth centuries AD. Tradition relates that two officials at the court of the emperor Constantine II (reigned 337–40) lived in a house on this site. Their names were John (Giovanni) and Paul (Paolo) and both were martyred under Julian the Apostate, the fourth-century emperor (and husband of Constantine's younger daughter) who tried to drag a largely Christianised Rome back to the worship of the pagan pantheon. Many of the rooms brought to light by the excavations here are remarkable for their wall-paintings, particularly those in the so-called confessio, approached up an iron stairway. Three figures are shown blindfolded and awaiting execution (*illustrated above*): this is thought to be the earliest extant depiction of a martyrdom.

From Santi Giovanni e Paolo, cross the little park of the Villa Celimontana to come out at Santa Maria in Domnica, on the summit of the Caelian Hill.

Santa Maria in Domnica

Map p. 301, C1 or p. 303, E4. Open 9–12.30 & 4.30–7.30.
This is an ancient church, standing on the highest point of the Caelian Hill. It is also commonly known as Santa Maria della Navicella, after the ancient Roman stone boat (probably a votive offering from soldiers at the nearby Castra Peregrina, a barracks for non-Romans) that was placed here by Cardinal Giovanni de' Medici, the future Pope Leo X, when he rebuilt the church in the sixteenth century. It still stands outside the church today, and now functions as a fountain.

Inside the church, all eyes immediately turn to the lovely mosaics on the triumphal arch and apse, dating from the ninth-century restoration of Pope Paschal I. On the arch sits Christ in Judgement, robed in gold with the orb of the earth between his feet, holding a scroll and flanked by angels and the apostles dressed in purple-fringed togas. Paul is the first apostle on the left, Peter the first on the right, with Moses and Elijah below them. In the conch are the Virgin and Child enthroned. Kneeling at the Virgin's feet, with a square halo to indicate that he was still alive at the time that this mosaic was made, is Pope Paschal. The Madonna and Child are flanked by angels, the blue of their haloes creating a striking abstract

'Dominus Firmamentum': The Lord is my strength.

pattern on either side. The whole is rendered against a lovely green ground, the colour of new spring grass, covered with white and red flowers. The monogram of Paschal is in the centre of the underside of the arch.

The coffered ceiling dates from the late sixteenth century. It was commissioned by another member of the Medici family, Ferdinando, later Grand Duke of Tuscany, who was titular cardinal of this church. Its central motif shows the Navicella (*illustrated opposite*), playing the part both of the Ark of Noah and of the Ark of the Host, the tabernacle which holds the Communion bread.

Santo Stefano Rotondo

Map p. 303, E4. Open Tues–Sat 9.30–12.30 & 2–5.

In AD 64, during the reign of Nero, a great fire consumed central Rome. It was witnessed by the emperor from a tower on the Esquiline Hill. After the flames had done their worst, Nero instigated a full-scale witch-hunt of the city's Christians: St Peter may have died at this time. Nero then expropriated the land in the valley between the Esquiline and Palatine hills and constructed his vast Domus Aurea, or Golden House, a sumptuous gilded pleasure palace whose grounds incuded a vast artificial lake (where the Colosseum stands now). To feed this lake, water was brought by a new aqueduct, parts of which can still be seen around St John Lateran and here on the Caelian Hill, in the gardens of Villa Celimontana. To get to the church of Santo Stefano Rotondo, you must pass close to some of its archways.

Santo Stefano Rotondo is a fascinating and atmospheric building, secretive and little-visited, is one of the finest surviving Roman examples of a circular mausoleum-church. It richly rewards any effort made to seek it out.

The association of a circular design with funeral architecture is very old, going back to the ancient Greeks and

the Etruscans. Imperial-era Rome made use of it too: the circular mausolea of Augustus and Hadrian still exist, one on either side of the Tiber. It is no surprise, then, that the tradition was also adopted by Christians. But just as Christian churches are congregational—unlike pagan temples, where access was restricted only to an elect college of priests—so Christian mausolea were also designed to accommodate crowds of the faithful. The mausolea of Augustus and Hadrian are mainly solid, with just a narrow tunnel and sepulchral chamber inside. There is no internal volume. Christian mausolea enclosed a wide open space designed to allow worshippers to process around and pay homage to the tomb within. The Church of the Holy Sepulchre in Jerusalem, built by Constantine around the tomb of Jesus, is the most famous example of such a structure. In Rome there is the partially collapsed mausoleum of St Helen, Constantine's mother; the mausoleum of her grand-daughter Constantia (the church of Santa Costanza); and this church, Santo Stefano Rotondo.

Santo Stefano dates from the late fifth century and is dedicated to the first Christian martyr, St Stephen. In the late sixteenth century the walls were decorated with scenes of the whole panoply of Christian martyrdom, beginning with the Massacre of the Innocents and the Passion of Christ and from there progressing to all the martyred saints, from Peter and Paul during the reign of Nero through all the gory deaths inflicted under subsequent imperial persecutors, and ending with a final scene showing a row of triumphant saints resurrected in peace and glory from the scenes of earthly carnage behind them.

The chapel on the left as you enter the church is dedicated to two Roman brothers, Primus and Felicianus, both martyred under Diocletian and buried in the old sandpits (*arenaria*) beside the Via Nomentana. Their remains were transferred here in the seventh century, from which time the chapel mosaics date. In the apse, the two saints are shown on either side of a jewelled cross with Christ in a roundel above it (not Christ crucified; for early attitudes to crucifixion, see p. 117). The sixteenth-century frescoes (*example illustrated on previous page*) show the two brothers exposed to lions and bears in the arena before being gruesomely done to death.

Below the church is a Mithraeum belonging to the Castra Peregrina barracks (*see p. 129; for the cult of Mithras, see p. 140*).

Santi Quattro Coronati
Map p. 303, E4. Open 9.30–12 & 4.30–6, Sun 9–10.40 & 4–5.45. Hours subject to change.

The convent of the Santi Quattro Coronati, the Four Crowned Saints, lies on an outlying spur of the Caelian Hill. It is home to a closed order of Augustinian nuns. You climb a steep, narrow road to reach their fawn-coloured brick and plaster fastness. The church, at the far end of the nunnery courtyard, is an early fourth-century foundation in honour of four Roman soldiers and five stonemasons from the province of Pannonia (modern Hungary) who refused to worship idols. It was enlarged and embellished by Honorius I and, after destruction by the Normans, was rebuilt on a smaller scale by Paschal II.

To view the Chapel of St Sylvester, with its famous frescoes, you need to apply at the barred window in the room to the right of the courtyard (ring the bell). The panel behind the bars is opened, you proffer your donation, and the chapel lights will be switched on. As the panel closes and the nun disappears again into her cloistered world,

Gerard Manley Hopkins's poem comes vividly to mind:

> I have desired to go
> Where springs not fail,
> To fields where flies no sharp and sided hail
> And a few lilies blow.
>
> And I have asked to be
> Where no storms come,
> Where the green swell is in the havens dumb,
> And out of the swing of the sea.

The Chapel of St Sylvester was decorated in 1246 with a fresco cycle illustrating a fictitious but charming sequence of events in the sainted pope's life, including the alleged baptism of Constantine by Pope Sylvester and Constantine's reciprocal gift in the form of a papal title to primacy over temporal princes. For the popes of the Middle Ages, embattled as they were, with Byzantine Christendom opposing them on the one hand and Holy Roman Emperors repeatedly inciting their people to insurrection on the other, it was important to demonstrate that both claims had substance.

The scenes occupy the middle band of the wall decoration and begin on the entrance wall in the left corner:

1: Constantine enthroned, with the trappings of princely power, but marred by spiritual and physical sickness.

The spots on his body show that he is suffering from leprosy;

2: The sick emperor, asleep, dreams of St Peter and St Paul who, stretching forth their arms to him, suggest that he seeks the aid of Pope Sylvester;

3: Three mounted messengers ride off to find the pope;

4: The messengers climb to the pope's mountain hermitage;

5: The pope returns to Rome and shows the emperor the painted likenesses of St Peter and St Paul;

6: Constantine is baptised by Pope Sylvester (*see illustration opposite*);

7: Cured of leprosy and born anew by water and the spirit, the grateful emperor presents his imperial tiara

Two important scenes from the fresco cycle of the life of Pope Sylvester (1246). Top: The Baptism of Constantine by Pope Sylvester. Bottom: The Donation of Constantine. Constantine was not baptised in Rome or by Pope Sylvester, nor did he give the papacy explicit or implicit badges of temporal office. The 'Donation' was a forgery probably from the eighth or ninth century which claimed to show that Constantine had given the Bishop of Rome dominion over all Italy. It was used to bolster papal claims to temporal power.

to the pope. This scene is a symbolic representation of the famous 'Donation of Constantine' (*see illustration and caption on previous page*);

8: The pope rides off wearing the tiara, led by Constantine;

9: The pope brings back to life a wild bull;

10: The finding of the True Cross by Constantine's mother, St Helen;

11: Almost entirely perished: the scene showed the pope liberating the Romans from a dragon.

San Clemente

Map p. 303, E3. Open 9–12.30 & 3–6; Sun and holidays 12–6.

San Clemente is one of the most interesting churches in the city. It is dedicated to St Clement, the fourth pope, who was martyred c. 99. The house on this site, over which the church was built, was a *domus* belonging to a certain Clemens, but probably not the pope (*see below*).

The San Clemente that is visited today exists on three levels: the level of today's functioning church; the earlier church below that; and the ancient remains yet one level further down.

The modern church

Even the 'modern' church preserves works of great beauty and antiquity. At the west end is the Chapel of St Catherine, with frescoes of her legendary life and martyrdom by the great early fifteenth-century Tuscan painter Masolino. The raised choir and its furnishings date from the sixth century. In the apse is a lovely twelfth-century mosaic, in striking colours of gold and dark blue, showing the crucified Christ in the centre, flanked by the Virgin and St John. The base of the Cross is smothered in acanthus leaves, from whose roots gush streams of living water at which deer quench their thirst. From the acanthus clump springs an immense, coiling Tree of Life, which fills the entire apse around the Cross and is inhabited by a vast collection of birds and other creatures. The Cross itself is decorated with twelve white doves symbolising the Apostles. The sheep below represent the flock of the faithful.

The lower church

This ancient church (*entry fee*), the scene of two fifth-century ecclesiastical councils, was destroyed by the Normans when they sacked Rome in 1084. Twenty years later Pope Paschal II removed its surviving furnishings and built a new church above the ruins. For centuries the old church lay buried and forgotten, until 1857, when the prior of the adjoining Irish Dominican friary rediscovered it. At the bottom of the entrance steps, on the wall on the right, is an eleventh-century fresco of the legend of St Clement.

He was allegedly banished to the Crimea, where he was thrown into the sea with an anchor tied to him, and buried in an underwater grave. He is the author of an epistle to the Corinthians, in which he rebukes them at length for the in-fighting which has broken out among them.

The ancient Roman remains

As you turn the corner at the bottom of the stairway that leads down to the third level, you will see, on your left, a Mithraic triclinium, or hall for ritual feasts. Mithraism was a mystery cult which originated in Persia and centred on ideas of sacrifice, fertility and redemption from darkness into light. Its adherents were all male. It was widely diffused in the Roman world, and indeed rivalled Christianity in popularity before Christianity became the state religion. Opposite the triclinium is the entrance porch of a Mithraic temple. A door to the left leads into a first-century Roman house thought to have belonged to the family of Flavius Clemens, a cousin of Domitian. Clement, the future pope and saint, may have begun life as a freedman in Clemens' household, since freedmen often took the names of their former masters.

TRASTEVERE

Trastevere, the district 'across the Tiber', is an atmospheric residential area, its narrow cobbled streets filled with restaurants, bars and little workshops. In ancient Roman times it was predominantly a Jewish district, and those members of the community who were converted to Christianity (the converted Jews were Rome's first Christians) had meeting houses here. Some churches of very early foundation survive.

San Crisogono

Map. p. 302, B3. Open 7.30–11.30 & 4–6.30.

San Crisogono is one of those churches—of which there are many in Rome—where you find out sooner who paid for its restoration and restructuring than in whose honour it was originally dedicated. It is preceded by a great porch, loudly blazoned with lettering, crying out to the world, the trams, the pigeons, the passers by, that Cardinal Scipione Borghese was responsible, in 1626.

Inside, it has a fine Cosmatesque floor pleasantly worn into little hills and valleys, plateaux and ridges, by generations of feet. Scipione Borghese's winged dragon emblem occurs in mosaic in the nave, replacing some of the original porphyry roundels. His name crops up again above the west door and over the chancel arch. His emblem in gilt wood is fixed twice to the ceiling. What of St Chrysogonus? Martyred under Diocletian, his relics are discreetly hidden away under the high altar.

The church that is dedicated to him, a very fine one, stands on the site of one of the oldest *tituli* in this part of Rome. The extensive remains of that older church lie under the present building (the entrance is at the end of the north aisle, through the vestry). They include traces of old flooring, fragments of frescoed wall including the scene of a stern St Benedict healing a leper in what was once the south aisle, and a collection of ancient sarcophagi, including one very fine one with the head of the deceased in a scallop shell surrounded by a marine revel.

Santa Maria in Trastevere

Map p. 302, A3. Open 7–7.30.

This beautiful church stands on a wide, lively square in central Trastevere. It is approached under a portico whose walls are covered with lapidary fragments, some of them pagan, some early Christian and others medieval. The main door announces: *Haec est porta Domini, justi intrabunt in eam*: 'This is the gate of the Lord, the just shall enter in by it'. Just or unjust, you go in at the side. But before you do, look up at the top of the main door to see the roundel of the Virgin and the Greek letters ΜΗΘΥ, standing for *Meter Theou*, 'Mother of God'. After Mary was declared to be the Mother of God at the Council of Ephesus in 431, her cult spread widely, and Santa Maria in Trastevere claims to be the earliest Marian church in Rome (a claim which is contested by the papal basilica of Santa Maria Maggiore). Motifs of Mary are prominent everywhere. On the exterior, her likeness appears at the very top of the bell-tower and also in the centre of the mosaic frieze on the façade, where she is depicted nursing the infant Jesus, with a procession of ten sumptuously-clad women bearing lamps on either side of her. Two of the women are veiled (the others are wearing crowns) and their lamps are unlit. The significance of this is still uncertain and is a subject of scholarly debate.

The glory of the interior is the apse, which has a fine mosaic in the conch dating from the twelfth century. Christ is shown enthroned with the Virgin. Above them a hand from Heaven presents a wreath; below is a frieze of Christ the Lamb with his twelve disciples as the sheep of his flock. On the triumphal arch, on either side, are the prophets Isaiah and Jeremiah bearing scrolls. On Isaiah's is written: *Ecce virgo concipiet et pariet filium*: 'Behold a virgin shall conceive and bear a son'. On Jeremiah's is written: *Dominus Christus captus est in peccatis nostris*: 'Christ the Lord is a prisoner of our sins'. Above each prophet hangs a caged bird, symbol of Christ confined by our transgression. Below them and all around the apse between the windows, are mosaic scenes of the life of the Virgin by the painter and mosaicist Pietro Cavallini, whose best surviving work of secure attribution is here and in the convent of the church of St Cecilia, also in Trastevere (*see below*). The scenes that are easiest to see are those immediately under the two prophets, of the birth and dormition of the Virgin. In the dormition scene, the Virgin's soul is shown rising up in the form of a swaddled child.

At the end of the north aisle is the precious icon of the *Madonna della Clemenza*, the Madonna of Mercy.

Santa Cecilia

Map p. 302, B4. Open 9.30–1 & 4–7.15. Excavations below the church close half an hour earlier. The Cavallini frescoes are shown Mon–Sat 10.15–12.15 and Sun 11.15–12.15.

The church of St Cecilia stands in a quiet part of Trastevere. The entrance opens off a cobbled square, taking you into a spacious, secluded courtyard planted with rose bushes and palms, oleander and bougainvillea, and with a fountain in the centre. Caecilia was a patrician Roman lady, martyred in 230 and buried in the Catacombs of San Callisto. In the ninth century her relics were discovered by Pope Paschal I, who had them transferred here, to the basilica he built on the foundations of her former house. A corridor leading off the south aisle (closed at the time of going to press; the lintel over the entrance is inscribed: *Cubiculum et oratorium divae Caeciliae*) leads to the remains of the bath house where she was condemned to be scalded to death. This manner of execution failed and she was beheaded instead (though her legend states that it was a botched job and that she lingered on in agony for three days). In 1599 her remains were rediscovered, miraculously intact. The sculptor Stefano Maderno witnessed the opening of her tomb. It contained a woman's body lying on its side, the head almost severed from the neck by a deep gash, and covered in a sere cloth. Maderno's famous and beautiful replica of what he saw, made of pure white Parian marble, now lies beneath the

Stefano Maderno's beautiful marble sculpture of St Cecilia, shown incorrupt, as she was discovered in 1599.

high altar. Above, in the apse, are mosaics commissioned by Pope Paschal, commemorating his discovery of the relics and depicting himself with a square halo, a sign that he was alive when the mosaics were made. The vivid blue of his halo is a hallmark of all Paschaline mosaics, as is his own monogram, which appears on the underside of the arch, aligned with the hand of God reaching out from the Heavens, and the halo of Christ, who is blessing in the Greek manner (thumb and ring finger joined to form a circle). Below Christ and the procession of saints, twelve sheep representing the apostles emerge from the holy cities of Bethlehem and Jerusalem to stand on either side of the Lamb, whose turquoise halo incorporates the Chi Rho. Paschal holds a model of his church. Directly above his head, perched in the branches of one of the two palm trees, sits a phoenix, symbol of resurrection and immortality.

The entrance to the crypt and archaeological remains beneath the church is from the north aisle (*entry fee*).

The Cavallini frescoes

These are in the convent attached to the church (*separate entrance; ring the bell at the door to the left of the church; entry fee; for opening times, see above*). A nun will accompany you in the lift to the chapel on the first floor. The chapel overlooks the church nave, its windows covered in perforated lead screens to allow the nuns to observe services without themselves being observed. On the wall opposite the windows is a splendid scene of Christ Enthroned, flanked by angels, the Virgin and John the Baptist and a procession of saints. Christ is displaying his wounds. Pietro Cavallini, painter and mosaicist, was one of the finest masters working in Rome in the late thirteenth century. On the entrance wall of the chapel is a fragmentary *Annunciation*.

San Francesco a Ripa

Map p. 302, B4. Open 7–12 & 4–7.30.

Not only were St Peter and St Paul in Rome together, but so were the founders of the two great mendicant orders of friars, St Francis of Assisi and St Dominic, who probably met each other in Rome in around 1217. St Dominic and his brethren had their church and friary at Santa Sabina on the Aventine; St Francis stayed here in Trastevere, in a hospice on the site of the church of San Francesco a Ripa. You approach his former room through the church sacristy, with its fine wood-panelled walls, under an old clock (still in working order). The cell preserves a stone which St Francis is said to have used as a pillow. The garden of the adjoining friary boasts a Seville orange tree reputed to have been planted by the saint (not to be out-done, incidentally, the cloister of Santa Sabina also boasts an orange tree, planted by St Dominic).

Admirers of Bernini come to San Francesco a Ripa for the Altieri Chapel, at the end of the north side, which contains the artist's monument to the Blessed Ludovica Albertoni (d. 1533), who dedicated much of her life to the poor of this parish. Ludovica died of an ague at the age of sixty. Bernini's effigy shows a much younger woman, writhing on a bed in an attitude of agonisingly ecstatic ambivalence.

ADVENTUS SIGERICI
AD ROMAM
ON THE TRAIL OF ARCHBISHOP SIGERIC

An *adventus*, in the days of imperial Rome, was the solemn and ceremonial entry into a city by the emperor, accompanied with all pomp and with public acclamations. Archbishop Sigeric, an Anglo Saxon cleric, former monk at Glastonbury, probably entered the city more quietly. Nevertheless, he was on an important mission.

Sigeric was born in about 940. Appointed Archbishop of Canterbury in 989, he came personally to Rome the following year to receive the pallium, the episcopal stole and formal token of his investiture, from the hands of Pope John XV[10].

Sigeric set off from Canterbury, either on foot or on horseback, to begin the arduous tramp to Rome along the Via Francigena, the pilgrim route across France and northern Italy. When the English travel writer H.V. Morton arrived in Rome in the 1950s by aeroplane, he felt it 'preposterous to be speeding through the sky...unaware of the great barrier which awed and terrified our ancestors.'

---

10   The pallium is still worn by the pope and archbishops. It is a narrow circular stole worn around the shoulders, with lappets hanging down in front and behind. It is made from the wool of white lambs blessed by the pope in the church of Sant'Agnese fuori le Mura (*see p. 154*).

The jagged peaks of the Alps near the Great St Bernard Pass, a redoubtable natural barrier between northern Europe and Rome.

He meant the Alps, the formidable blockade between Italy and northern Europe. Sigeric certainly crossed them. We don't know whether he felt any awe or terror but we do have a record of what he did when he was in Rome and of his return journey to England. It survives, in manuscript form, in the British Library in London. Sigeric wasn't a pilgrim as such: he hadn't come to save his soul with a papal blessing. But he did undertake an arduous, flat-out tour of twenty-three churches when he was in the Holy City. The text of the Latin manuscript translates as follows:

> The arrival of Sigeric our archbishop in Rome. First to the sanctuary of St Peter the Apostle. Then to St Mary of the English College. To St Lawrence in Craticula. To St Valentine at the Milvian Bridge. To St Agnes. To St Lawrence outside the Walls. To St Se-

bastian. To St Anastasius. To St Paul. To St Boniface.
To St Sabina. To St Mary of the Greek College. To St
Cecilia. To St Chrysogonus. To St Mary across the Tiber. To St Pancras. Then they returned to their lodging. The next day to St Mary Rotunda. To the Holy
Apostles. To St John Lateran. There we took refresh-
ment with Pope John. Then to Jerusalem. To St Mary
Major. To St Peter ad Vincula. To St Lawrence where
his body was roasted.

All but one of those churches still exist and it is possible
to retrace Sigeric's footsteps. The churches can be identified as follows:

1. 'St Peter the Apostle'.
This is the basilica of **St Peter's** (*described on p. 70*).

2. 'St Mary of the English College'.
The church of **Santo Spirito in Sassia** (*map p. 300, C2;
open 7–12 & 3–7.30*) is in the Borgo, the Vatican suburb
where hospices and religious communities flourished in
the Middle Ages. In the early eighth century, Ine, King of
Wessex, founded a chapel and hospice for Anglo Saxon
pilgrims and clerics. If he was not staying in the papal
guest house next to St Peter's—which from the fifteenth
century onwards would be transformed and remodelled
as the Vatican Palace—Sigeric may have had his lodging
here. The name Sassia (sometimes written Saxia) derives

from the Latin and Italian words for Saxon. On the south side of the church today is the deeply venerated altar of the Sacred Heart of Jesus, blessed by Pope John Paul II in 1995, with a striking altarpiece of Divine Mercy streaming from Christ's heart in a blinding prism of light.

3. 'St Lawrence in Craticula'.
From the point of view of geography, it would make sense if this were the church of San Lorenzo in Piscibus, the back of which can be seen from Borgo Santo Spirito (*map p. 300, C2*). San Lorenzo in Craticola, however, was a name given to the church of **San Lorenzo in Lucina**, just off the Corso (*map p. 302, C1; described on p. 184*), because it preserves a relic of the *craticula*, or gridiron, on which St Lawrence is said to have been martyred.

4. 'St Valentine at the Milvian Bridge'.
The true identity of St Valentine is obscure, though one tradition makes him an early bishop martyred on the Via Flaminia, the continuation of the Corso which runs north from Rome, on 14th February 273. His remains were buried nearby. The spot soon became a Christian burial ground, and an adjoining basilica was built in the fourth century. It flourished until St Valentine's relics were taken into the centre of the city, to the church of Santa Maria in Cosmedin (*see p. 157*). At the time, this so-called 'translation' of relics was common practice. The emperor Theodosius I had passed a series of acts between 378 and

St Valentine with the attribute of his martyrdom, the axe. The book he holds bears a text from John 13:'Love one another as I have loved you'. The theme of love and faithfulness, with which Valentine is chiefly associated today, is taken up in the pair of mating birds upon the tree stump.

380 declaring Christianity the official religion of the empire. In the West the emperor Gratian, encouraged by Ambrose, Bishop of Milan, set about suppressing paganism in his portion of the realm. Christianity triumphed. A century later, Christians began to overcome their aversion to pagan associations, adapting buildings in central Rome as churches, consecrated by the bones of martyrs brought in by the barrow-load from the old, outlying burial sites.

St Valentine's original basilica exists only as a ruin, attached to catacombs dug into the Parioli hill, at Viale Maresciallo Pilsudski 2 (close to where it meets Via di San Valentino). Traditionally the site was open to the public on St Valentine's Day, but the complex is extremely unstable: of the basilica that had been enlarged and embellished by that tireless beautifier of martyrs' shrines, Pope Honorius I, nothing at all remains to be seen.

A little further north, however, in the Olympic Village built for the summer games of 1960, there is the modern church of **San Valentino**, consecrated in 1986 (*map p. 9; corner of Viale Diciasettesima Olimpiade and Via Germania; bus 217 from Termini Station*). This is a remote location, and on the feast day of the saint, few seek out his church. Millions are scurrying around with cellophane-wrapped flowers, and blood-red fluffy hearts are dangling in every gift-shop window. But in the church of St Valentine only a subdued Mass is taking place in a side room. The spirit of the saint lives on in the tradition whereby lovers attach padlocks to the nearby Milvian Bridge as a symbol of their indivisible attachment to each other (*see p. 201*). The association of St Valentine with lovers comes from the date of his martyrdom, 14th February, the day when, according to old lore, mating birds choose their nesting partners.

5. 'St Agnes'.
By this Sigeric means the minor basilica of **Sant'Agnese fuori le Mura** (*described on p. 162*).

THE LAMBS OF ST AGNES & THE PALLIUM

Archbishop Sigeric made his journey to Rome to receive the pallium, his stole of office, from Pope John XV. During his time here, he visited three churches intimately connected with the manufacture of this vestment, a connection which is still maintained to this day.

Every year, two winter lambs are purchased from the Cistercian monks of Santi Vincenzo e Anastasio at Tre Fontane. It is their wool that will be used to make the pallia. On the feast of St Agnes (21st January), the two lambs are taken to the basilica of Sant'Agnese fuori le Mura and solemnly blessed. The association of St Agnes with lambs comes from a play on the virgin martyr's name (Agnes) and the Latin word for a lamb (*agnus*). If the pope is not present at the service, then the lambs are afterwards taken to the Vatican, decked in white roses, to receive his benediction. After this they are entrusted to the care of the Benedictine sisters of the convent of Santa Cecilia in Trastevere, where they are raised with the utmost care until Holy Week, when they are shorn. The nuns weave their wool into the pallia which will be conferred on new metropolitan archbishops on the Feast of St Peter and St Paul (29th June). In the apse mosaic of Santa Cecilia in Trastevere, Pope Paschal I is shown wearing the pallium. His is pure white, adorned with two red crosses.

6. 'St Lawrence outside the Walls'.
San Lorenzo fuori le Mura (*described on p. 98*).

7. 'St Sebastian'.
San Sebastiano on the Via Appia (*described on p. 101*).

8. 'St Anastasius'.
Santi Vincenzo e Anastasio at Tre Fontane (*described on p. 42*).

9. 'St Paul'.
San Paolo fuori le Mura (*described on p. 45*).

10. 'St Boniface'.
Sant'Alessio on the Aventine (*described on p. 120*), which was dedicated to St Boniface until 1217.

11. 'St Sabina'.
Santa Sabina (*described on p. 116*).

12. 'St Mary of the Greek College'.
Sigeric now descended from Santa Sabina to the foot of the Aventine Hill, close to the Tiber bank (it is tempting to imagine him coming down the cobbled Clivo di Rocca Savella), to visit the beautiful and ancient church of **Santa Maria in Cosmedin** (*map p. 302, C4; open 9.30–4.50, until 5.40 in summer*). In ancient times this area was a market place and cattle dealers congregated around the

Arch of Janus. Barge-loads of goods would have arrived upriver from the port of Ostia. In fact it has been suggested (though not confirmed) that the ancient columned building which forms the framework of Santa Maria in Cosmedin was the Roman *statio annonae*, a distribution centre for the public grain supply. In early Christian times a welfare centre occupied the building, and it was converted into a church in the eighth century. This is the church that Sigeric would have seen: its interior layout, with its antique columns and the remains of the side wall of the ancient Roman building, is unchanged. The furnishings and decoration are of the twelfth century. The church preserves the skull of St Valentine, and other sundry parts of him, in a bronze and glass reliquary.

In the former sacristy, however, now the souvenir shop, there is a work of art which certainly existed in Sigeric's day, the gold-ground mosaic of the *Adoration of the Magi*, dating from 706. What survives is just a fragment (*illustrated opposite*): we see the Virgin seated on a cushioned, high-backed chair, the traditional gold stars (symbols of her virginity) clearly picked out on her forehead and shoulder, with Joseph behind her and an angel in front. The infant Jesus on her lap stretches out a hand to inspect the box of gold being proffered by one of the Magi (of whom only the left arm survives).

Underneath the church porch is fixed the famous **Bocca della Verità**, an ancient fountain-head placed here in 1632. A legend has grown up around it, claiming that its mouth will clamp shut on the hand of any perjurer placed inside it. People queue to test it out and to have their photo taken while doing so.

Today the church holds services according to the Melkite Uniate rite.

13. 'St Cecilia'.
Santa Cecilia (*described on p. 144*).

14. 'St Chrysogonus'.
San Crisogono (*described on p. 141*).

15. 'St Mary across the Tiber'.
Santa Maria in Trastevere (*described on p. 142*).

16. 'St Pancras'.
San Pancrazio (*described on p. 189*).

17. 'St Mary Rotunda'.
The Pantheon (*described on p. 217*).

18. 'The Holy Apostles'.
Santi Apostoli (*described on p. 166*).

19. **St John Lateran** (*described on p. 56*).
The fact that Sigeric and his retinue met the pope here is not surprising: until the fourteenth century the papal seat was in the Lateran Palace. Only after 1378 did they move to the Vatican. Sigeric and Pope John perhaps dined in the grand banqueting hall, decorated with mosaics from the time of Leo III and Charlemagne (*see p. 69*).

20. 'Jerusalem'.
Santa Croce in Gerusalemme (*described on p. 93*).

21. 'St Mary Major'.
Santa Maria Maggiore (*described on p. 86*).

22. 'St Peter ad Vincula'.
San Pietro in Vincoli (*described on p. 21*).

23. 'St Lawrence where his body was roasted'.

The church of **San Lorenzo in Panisperna** (*map p. 303, E2*) stands in a little square where four roads meet, behind an elaborate stairway and a gate decorated with a crown and a palm of martyrdom. This is the traditional site of the death of St Lawrence, a deacon of the early Church in Rome, on 10th August 258. According to tradition, he was roasted alive on a gridiron. A rather charming story holds that he remained defiant to the last, refusing to show his physical suffering, even to the extent of asking his executioners to turn him over, because 'I'm done on this side.'

DOMUS DEI, ECCLESIA DEI VIVI
NOTABLE ROMAN CHURCHES

'The house of the Lord, the church of the living God.'

1 Timothy 3:15

There are over nine hundred churches in Rome. Many are described at length in the preceding chapters. The following pages give a small additional selection of those which for various reasons are exceptional and worthy of any pilgrim's time. Some of them house venerated relics, some are the burial places of apostles, saints and martyrs. Others are very ancient, perhaps built upon the foundations of an early Christian *titulus* or *domus ecclesiae* (*see box on p. 122*). Some combine more than one of these distinctions. Still others are home to important works of art. They are described below in alphabetical order.

Sant'Agnese in Agone
Map p. 302, B2. Open Tues–Sat 9.30–12.30 & 4–7, Sun 10–1 & 4–8; closed Mon.

There are two churches in Rome dedicated to St Agnes, the girl martyr who was probably a victim of the persecutions of Diocletian in the early fourth century. Little is known for certain about her, though her cult is wide-

spread and popular, particularly in Rome, and it is generally agreed that she met her death at the age of twelve or
thirteen. According to tradition, she was exposed naked
in the Stadium of Domitian, the modern Piazza Navona.
Her hair miraculously grew long enough for her to wrap
around her body and thus cover herself modestly. According to other sources she was consigned to the flames
and remained unscathed; was sent to be deflowered in a
brothel but emerged intact (the man who looked on her
lustfully was struck blind); and was eventually beheaded,
before being laid to rest in a burial ground to the northeast of the city.

On the site of her exposure to the jeering multitude
now stands the splendid Baroque church of Sant'Agnese
in Agone, its grand façade a design of the 1650s by the
great architect Francesco Borromini. The name of the
church does not refer to the saint's 'agony'; it comes from
the word *agones*, meaning athletic games, a reference to
the contests that took place in the Stadium of Domitian
which once occupied this site and whose contours are
followed by the shape of Piazza Navona.

The interior seems somewhat squat after such a grand
façade. Nevertheless, it boasts a *tour-de-force* cupola fresco and altarpieces that are all sculpted in high relief. The
one on the right, by Bernini's assistant Ercole Ferrata,
shows St Agnes in the flames that would not burn her. As
if in anticipation of a victory declared, two angels above
her get ready with a wreath and a martyr's palm. A small

chapel entered from the north side contains the saint's tiny skull in a rather lovely silver casket.

As you leave the church, look up to bid adieu to Pope Innocent X, who leans out from a sculpted balcony, arm raised in hopeful benediction of a crowd that never loved him. It was Pope Innocent (Giovanni Battista Pamphilj) who ordered the remodelling of this church and the restoration of Piazza Navona to its present form, complete with Bernini's famous Fountain of the Four Rivers (Nile, Ganges, Danube and Rio della Plata). Innocent was an austere man, slow to make up his mind, scrupulously honest and thus difficult to deal with, and perceived by the public to be hag-ridden by his sister-in-law. He died unmourned. This funerary monument was erected three quarters of a century after his death.

Sant'Agnese fuori le Mura
Map p. 9. Via Nomentana 349. Bus 60 from Piazza Venezia and Via Nazionale to the XXI Aprile stop. Open Tues–Sat 7.30–12 & 4–7.30.

The other Roman church dedicated to St Agnes is the beautiful basilica of Sant'Agnese fuori le Mura, built above the virgin martyr's grave beside the Via Nomentana. St Agnes's relics are preserved in the catacombs below the church (*see p. 113*).

The church itself is extremely fine, austere without and solemnly beautiful within, as is the case with so many of

The Latin verse eulogy of St Agnes composed by Pope Damasus I and rendered in the particular script known as the Damasan Letters, with thick, stocky uprights and tiny little serifs like an insect's feelers. They are the work of the stonecarver Furius Dionysius Filocalus.

the early Christian basilicas. It was built in the seventh century by Pope Honorius I, who had instigated a programme of embellishing the tombs of martyrs.

Entrance is either by the west door or from the south side. The side entrance takes you down a flight of stairs whose walls are covered with early inscriptions. One of these, at the bottom on the right, is the verse eulogy of St Agnes composed by Pope Damasus I (*illustrated above and see also p. 183*). The Latin translates roughly as follows:

The story goes, according to the blessed parents, that when the trumpet had sounded its melancholy note, Agnes suddenly sprang from the lap of her nurse, voluntarily to trample upon the rage and threats of the rabid tyrant. Though he desired to scorch her noble body in the flames, with her slight strength she overcame great fear, and being naked spread her thick hair upon her limbs, that none might see the Temple of the Lord. O thou, worthy of my veneration, holy token of modesty, glorious martyr, give ear to the prayers of Damasus.

In the church interior, the focal point is the beautiful apse, clad in sober grey marble interspersed with strips of porphyry. The conch is filled with a seventh-century mosaic showing Agnes herself. A hand reaches down from the Heavens to place a coronet on her head. Beside her stands Pope Honorius, carrying a model of his basilica.

Nearby in the basilica complex is the earlier, very interesting church of Santa Costanza (*see p. 176*).

Sant'Agostino
Map 302, B1. Open 7.45–12 & 4.30–7.30.
This fine church, just outside Piazza Navona, is dedicated to St Augustine, the great theologian whose mother is buried here. The most famous work of art in the church is Caravaggio's *Madonna di Loreto*, or *Madonna dei Pellegrini*, in the first north chapel, commissioned for this altar in 1604 (coin-operated light). It shows the Virgin at the door of her house showing the infant Christ to two kneeling peasants who have come on a pilgrimage. The Child raises his right hand to them in blessing. When the painting was first unveiled, the peasants' dirty feet caused something of a stir: uncleanliness of this kind was not thought a fit subject for a church altarpiece.

The nave has frescoes of the prophets: the Prophet Isaiah, on the third north pillar, is by Raphael. At the west end by the entrance door is the *Madonna del Parto* by the Florentine artist Jacopo Sansovino (1521), a statue to whom expectant mothers traditionally offer prayers of thanks and hope for safe delivery.

The tomb of St Monica, mother of Augustine, can be found in the chapel to the left of the choir. Monica was born in North Africa, where she lived as the tirelessly patient wife of an unfaithful, violent-tempered pagan husband named Patricius (whom she won for Christianity shortly before his death). As a widow she followed her son to Italy, and it was through her that he was baptised (in Milan). In his *Confessions*, St Augustine writes: 'In the flesh she brought me to birth in this world: in her heart she brought me to birth in your eternal light.' (Tr. R.S. Pine-Coffin). She died in 387 in Ostia, where she had been waiting for a boat to take her and her son to Africa. Part of her tombstone is preserved there in the church of Santa Aurea (*see p. 226*). Her relics were transferred to this church in the mid-fifteenth century, from which time the effigy dates, though the tomb-chest itself is said to be the original.

Sant'Alfonso
Map p. 303, F2. Open 7–7.30.
Very close to Santa Maria Maggiore, the busy Via Merulana meets Via San Vito, which leads to the picturesque-

ly precarious-looking Arch of Gallienus (first century), the ancient Esquiline Gate, beyond which lay a tract of ground reserved for crucifixions. At the point where Via San Vito and Via Merulana meet is the sanctuary church of Sant'Alfonso. Its steps are occupied by the statutory mendicant, scrupulously guarding his (or her) patch; its interior, in chilly weather, offers sanctuary and a roof to the homeless of the district. It is also home to a precious icon of the Cretan-Byzantine school, known as the *Madonna del Perpetuo Soccorso*. The Madonna is shown holding the infant Christ in a protective embrace, as if trying to shield him from his ultimate destiny, which is betokened by the archangels Michael and Gabriel who hover in the background, one of them holding the Cross, the other the vinegar sponge. As if frightened by the sight of these portents of the Passion, the Child clasps his mother's thumb in both his tiny hands, and one of his sandals has fallen from his foot.

Santi Apostoli
Map p. 302, C2. Open 7–12 & 4–7.
This large church, very close to Piazza Venezia, is dedicated to the Twelve Apostles and is the resting place of two, St Philip and St James the Less. You descend to their tomb down a double curved stairway, under an arch surmounted by crossed palm branches and a Latin announcement, in black and gold mosaic: 'The bodies of the saints are entombed in peace; their names will live for ever'.

HIC CONDITA SVNT CORPORA SS. APOSTOLOR PHILIPPI ET IACOBI MIN

Detail of the tomb-chest that contains the relics of the apostles Philip and James the Less. The image is a reference to the Feeding of the Five Thousand, one of the famous gospel events at which Philip is named:

'When Jesus then lifted up his eyes, and saw a great company come unto him, he saith unto Philip, Whence shall we buy bread, that these may eat? And this he said to prove him: for he himself knew what he would do. Philip answered him, Two hundred pennyworth of bread is not sufficient for them, that every one of them may take a little. One of his disciples, Andrew, Simon Peter's brother, saith unto him, There is a lad here, which hath five barley loaves, and two small fishes: but what are they among so many? And Jesus said, Make the men sit down. Now there was much grass in the place. So the men sat down, in number about five thousand. And Jesus took the loaves; and when he had given thanks, he distributed to the disciples, and the disciples to them that were sat down; and likewise of the fishes as much as they would. When they were filled, he said unto his disciples, Gather up the fragments that remain, that nothing be lost. Therefore they gathered them together, and filled twelve baskets with the fragments of the five barley loaves, which remained over and above unto them that had eaten.'

John 6: 5–13

The whole area is painted to resemble an ancient Roman house. The relics of the saints are contained within a pretty tomb-chest (*illustrated above*).

In the south aisle there is a monument to Clementina Sobieska, wife of James Stuart, the Old Pretender, and mother of Bonnie Prince Charlie. Palazzo Balestra in the square outside (the orange building) was presented to the couple as a wedding gift by Pope Clement XI. Bonnie Prince Charlie was born there.

Three other works of art are worthy of note, two of them by the great Neoclassical sculptor Canova. The first is the monument to Pope Clement XIV, which forms the surround to the sacristy door at the end of the north aisle, and which shows the pope raising his hand to bless all those who enter. The other is in the porch, a monument to Giovanni Volpato. At the opposite end of the porch is a second-century relief of a Roman imperial eagle, found in the Forum of Trajan.

San Bartolomeo
Map p. 302, B3. Open 9.30–1 & 3.30–7, Sun 9–1.
The Isola Tiberina, the island in the Tiber, has been associated with works of healing since the third century BC, when a sacred snake, brought to Rome from the sanctuary of Asclepius in Epidaurus, Greece, escaped from its basket and slithered there. Its choice of abode was seen as portentous and a temple was built, dedicated to Asclepius, god of medicine, whom the Romans knew as Aesculapius.

In the imperial period, we learn from Suetonius, tight-fisted masters would abandon sick and worn-out slaves on this island, in the self-exonerating hope that Aesculapius would take care of them—but in truth so that they themselves would not be troubled by medical bills. The island today is home to a large hospital, and the site of the ancient temple is now occupied by a church dedicated to St Bartholomew the Apostle, whose relics it claims.

On a sunny day the Tiber island is a pleasant place to picnic and sunbathe, on the wide, stone-faced southern shore. You approach the island by a choice of two ancient Roman footbridges, Ponte Fabricio or Ponte Cestio, both dating from the first century BC. From the island's southern tip you have a good view of another ancient bridge, the Ponte Rotto or 'Broken Bridge', now reduced to a single arch. These are the sole remains of the *Pons Aemilius*, built in the second century BC.

The much-weathered travertine facing of the buildings at this end of the island still preserves the contours of a relief sculpture of Aesculapius himself. The face has perished but you can still make out his shoulder, arm and staff, with the serpent coiled around it.

The church of San Bartolomeo announces in Latin on its façade that, 'In this basilica rests the body of St Bartholomew the Apostle'. The relics lie enclosed within the high altar, which is formed of a beautiful porphyry basin from the Baths of Caracalla. The well-head in the centre of the chancel steps, carved in the medieval period with figures of Christ and St Bartholomew, is thought to stand above the site of a healing spring connected to the ancient temple of Aesculapius.

Very little is known about St Bartholomew. He is mentioned four times in scripture: three times in the Gospels and once in Acts, in lists along with the other disciples. Tradition says that he was flayed alive, possibly in Armenia, from where his remains found their way first to the island of Lipari, off the Sicilian coast, then to southern Italy and thence to Rome. In art, Bartholomew is often depicted with a flaying knife. In his *Last Judgement* in the Sistine Chapel, Michelangelo famously chose to show Bartholomew holding his own skin. Although not in itself a new idea, what makes Michelangelo's work different is that the sagging face reveals a clear self-portrait of the artist.

Some scholars believe Bartholomew to be the same person as Nathanael, the friend of Philip, whose calling is mentioned in the Gospel of John (the only gospel writer who does not mention a Bartholomew):

Now Philip was of Bethsaida, the city of Andrew and Peter. Philip findeth Nathanael, and saith unto him, 'We have found him, of whom Moses in the law, and the prophets, did write, Jesus of Nazareth, the son of Joseph.'

And Nathanael said unto him, 'Can any good thing come out of Nazareth?'

Philip saith unto him, 'Come and see.'

Jesus saw Nathanael coming to him, and saith of him, 'Behold an Israelite indeed, in whom is no guile!'

Nathanael saith unto him, 'Whence knowest thou me?'

Jesus answered and said unto him, 'Before Philip called thee, when thou wast under the fig tree, I saw thee.'

Nathanael answered and saith unto him, 'Rabbi, thou art the Son of God; thou art the King of Israel.'

Jesus answered and said unto him, 'Because I said unto thee, I saw thee under the fig tree, believest thou? Thou shalt see greater things than these.' And he saith unto him, 'Verily, verily, I say unto you, Hereafter ye shall see heaven open, and the angels of God ascending and descending upon the Son of man.' *John 1:44–51*

The altarpiece behind the high altar, in the form of an icon, is sacred to all twentieth-century martyrs, to whom the church was dedicated by Pope John Paul II in the Holy Year of 2000. The church is also the headquarters of the Comunità di Sant'Egidio, a lay Catholic missionary community dedicated to helping the needy. It is known particularly for its work with HIV and AIDS.

Chiesa Nuova

Map p. 302, A2. Open 7.30–12 & 4.30–7.15; Sun and holidays 8–1 & 4.30–7.15.

St Philip Neri is one of the most attractive figures of the Counter-Reformation, a man of immense kindness and good humour, prodigiously partial to snuff, known for his work among the sick and the destitute of Rome, and for such positive-thinking mottoes as 'Cheerfulness strengthens the heart'. In 1548 he founded the Confraternity of the Most Holy Trinity, with the twofold mission of caring for convalescents discharged from hospital but not yet strong enough to work, and assisting pilgrims of slender means. His Chiesa Nuova, 'New Church', was begun in 1575. The handles of its entrance doors are decorated with the motif of the flaming heart, the *cor flammigerum*, St Philip's emblem: in 1544 the saint had experienced a vision of a ball of flame entering his body through his mouth and causing his heart to become distended. When his corpse was examined prior to his canonisation, the physical effects of this were found to be discernible in the form of damage to the ribcage.

The church feels like a little island of peace. The growling buses and flatulent vespas on the Corso outside seem strangely remote. St Philip is buried here, in the chapel to the left of the sanctuary, where he lies beneath the altar in a glass casket, and where the faithful come to offer their respects.

The paintings in the sanctuary are by Rubens. The one on the right shows Domitilla, kinswoman of Domitian, and the two early martyrs Nereus and Achilleus, who were buried in the Catacombs of Domitilla (*see p. 110*).

The pediments on the confessionals are all in the characteristic 'peaked umbrella' shape which the architect Francesco Borromini so loved. This prepares you to appreciate the pale *café au lait*-coloured building which adjoins the church outside, facing the busy

Twin *cor flammigerum* door handles at Chiesa Nuova.

Corso, with its curvilinear façade and peaked umbrella pediment. This is Borromini's Oratory of St Philip, the prayer house where the saint and the members of his order met, and where concerts were given. It has lent its name to the form of musical composition known as the oratorio.

Santi Cosma e Damiano

Map p. 303, D3. Open 9–12 & 4–6.

Maxentius, rival of Constantine, whom the latter defeated and killed at the Battle of the Milvian Bridge in 312, had a son, Romulus, named after the founder of Rome, the city which Maxentius claimed as his capital. Romulus predeceased his father in 309 and a temple was erected in the Forum to the dead boy's memory, beside the vast basilica that Maxentius was having built (or so it was thought; other scholars believe that the dedication of this temple was to Jupiter Stator, Jupiter who gives staying-power in battle). Whoever the dedicatee, in the sixth century the temple dwindled to a mere vestibule or antechamber to the church of Santi Cosma e Damiano, dedicated to two brothers from Asia Minor who won fame as healers and who are now the patron saints of doctors. The church is no longer entered from the Forum—a pity, because the bronze doors are the fourth-century originals—but is approached from the busy road behind, Via dei Fori Imperiali.

The west end of the church has been glassed over so that you can look down into the ancient temple. At the east end, in the apse, is a splendid mosaic, commissioned by Pope Felix IV (reigned 526–30). The central scene shows Cosmas and Damian being presented to Christ by St Peter and St Theodore (right) and by St Paul and Pope Felix (left). Pope Felix carries a model of his church. Both Christ and St Paul have gammadia (*see opposite*) on their robes, the I (iota), first letter of the name Jesus in Greek. Christ is depicted as an ancient orator, his left hand holding a scroll, his right stretched forth in acclamation—but also pointing to the twinkling phoenix, symbol of resurrection, which perches in the branches of the palm tree. He is clad in a golden toga and appears before a vivid mackerel sky.

The first south altar has an eighth-century Byzantine *Christ Crucified*, shown robed and with open eyes.

GAMMADIA

The gammadion (plural: gammadia) is a Christological symbol commonly found in early mosaics. It takes the form of a Greek letter of the alphabet shown as if embroidered on the robes of Christ or the saints. In Italy, gammadia are commonly found in Rome, Milan and Ravenna. There is no consensus about what meaning these symbols are meant to convey. Some commentators have suggested that they are purely decorative. This seems unlikely. It is more credible to assume that the mosaicists had a purpose. Some of the more common gammadia have been interpreted as follows:

Γ: Gamma, the third letter, the Trinity, the Three-in-One, the corner-stone;

Ι: Iota, symbol of the Law and of the Word made flesh;

Ζ: Zeta, symbol of life (in Greek, Ζωή);

Η: Eta, corresponding to the number 8, a numeral associated with new beginnings (hence the popularity of octagonal baptisteries), also often interpreted as a gate, through which we may pass to new life;

Θ: Theta, corresponding to the number 9, signifying completion, fulfilment (it is also the first letter of the Greek word Θάνατος; death), the ninth hour at which Christ's soul left his body.

Santa Costanza

Map p. 9. Open Tues–Sat 9–12 & 4–6, Sun 4–6, Mon 9–12.
No trace remains of the early basilica of St Peter, nor of
that which was erected over the burial place of St Paul.
The earliest Roman church of all, St John Lateran, has
been altered out of all recognition. Successions of popes
and prelates, all desiring to leave behind them some tangible token of their piety and munificence, have seen to
it that these great churches have been rebuilt, enlarged,
embellished and reconstituted many times during the
course of their existence. For those wishing to gain a
sense of how the earliest churches looked, of what atmosphere and environment surrounded those first worshippers, there is no clue to be found in the major basilicas.
We must turn instead to churches like this one, the little
circular mausoleum of Constantia, elder daughter of the
emperor Constantine.

At some time between 337 and 350, not very many
years after her father had confessed the Christian faith,
Constantia built a cemetery basilica on her estate, next to
the tomb where the martyred St Agnes had been buried
in 304 and over which Pope Honorius I would later build
the church of Sant'Agnese (*see p. 162*). To the cemetery
basilica Constantia then joined a small mausoleum for
herself, so that the intercessions of pilgrims at the martyr's shrine might also benefit her own soul. That mausoleum was subsequently converted into a church and
survives today as the church of Santa Costanza—though

Constantia was never canonised, nor was her life a particularly saintly one. But both she and her younger sister Helena were buried here.

As you approach the mausoleum, on the right in a grassy area behind a modern fence, you will see what remains of the original cemetery basilica. The curved ends of the apsidal vestibule which linked the two buildings survive to right and left of the entrance door. The mausoleum is circular in plan. Originally it would have had a further exterior colonnade. The beautifully-preserved interior consists of an outer ambulatory separated from the central space by twenty-four paired granite columns with composite capitals (one of them is a pure Corinthian exception) taken from earlier buildings. On the barrel vaulting of the ambulatory are remarkable mosaics (fourth century), executed for a Christian purpose though pagan in character, designed in pairs on a white ground. Those flanking the entrance have a geometric design, and the next pair has roundels with animals and human figures. Scenes of the grape harvest and vine tendrils with grapes follow: this is pure pagan Dionysiac roistering, with cherubs treading grapes as if in a drunken dance. The fourth pair of mosaics has roundels with a leaf pattern, busts and figures. In the square niche opposite the entrance is a copy of Constantia's sarcophagus. The original magnificent porphyry tomb-chest is now in the Vatican Museums. The mosaics above the tomb to either side are of leaves, branches, amphorae and exotic birds.

Detail of the sarcophagus of Constantia, daughter of Constantine, preserved in the Vatican Museums. It features symbols that were popular in pagan times but which were also adopted by Christians: the acanthus frond as symbol of eternal life, the winged cherub, the lamb, the vine and grapes, and the peacock (to right and left at the bottom you can see a peacock's tail), a symbol of incorruptibility. Recent studies have suggested that this may in fact have been the sarcophagus of Constantia's sister Helena, the wife of the emperor Julian, known as the Apostate, who reverted to the pagan religion. He appears to have been devoted to his wife and remained unwed after her death. Perhaps he did indeed commission this splendid chest for her mortal remains. The motifs on this sarcophagus, as well as those in the vault mosaics of the mausoleum, led to the building being known as the Temple of Bacchus in the Middle Ages. Parties of revellers would make their drunken way there until the practice was suppressed by Pope Clement XI in the eighteenth century. A second sarcophagus from the masuoleum, also of porphyry but smaller, is now in St Peter's, host to the relics of the apostles Simon and Jude. It was traditionally thought to have been Helena's, but perhaps after all it was Constantia's.

Directly over the sarcophagus are fragments of a mosaic with a star design.

The two side niches have later mosaics (fifth or seventh century), interesting though somewhat crude, and much restored: on the left is a scene of the *Traditio Legis*, where Christ presents the scroll of the Law to St Peter, with St Paul on Christ's other side (he has the iota gammadion on his garments; *for gammadia, see p. 175*). On the scroll is written the legend, *Dominus pacem dat*: 'The Lord gives peace'. Below is a rich mosaic swag of pomegranates and bunches of grapes. On the right we see the *Traditio Clavium*, with Christ presenting the keys of Heaven to St Peter.

The Gesù

Map p. 302, C2. Open 6–12.30 & 4–7.15.

St Peter understood human nature. He knew that it is very difficult to believe in something, truly to believe it and to go on doing so, without tangible proof. In scripture we hear him make repeated reference to the fact that the wonders he relates are not fancies but things which he saw with his own eyes. They are not allegories, parables or metaphors. They are facts. 'This Jesus hath God raised up, whereof we all are *witnesses*.' (*Acts 2:32*); 'And we are *witnesses* of all things which he did both in the land of the Jews, and in Jerusalem; whom they slew and hanged on a tree.' (*Acts 10:39*).

Pope Nicholas V (reigned 1447–55) understood human nature too. Most men, he declared, 'lose their belief in the course of time, unless they are moved by certain extraordinary sights'. With this in mind he proceeded to put in hand the rebuilding and embellishing of St Peter's basilica, to make it appear to those who entered it like a veritable heaven on earth.

A century later, the popes and prelates of the Counter-Reformation fought tooth and nail against the reforms of Protestantism, with both extraordinary sights and extraordinary objects. They fully understood the power of relics, of Columns of the Flagellation, of hallowed spots where martyrs groaned their last, of tangible evidence that they really did do so. The sumptuous church of the Gesù, properly the Church of the Most Holy Name of Jesus, is the Jesuit church in Rome and it perfectly exemplifies the attitudes of the Counter-Reformation, of which the Jesuits were a driving force. It attempted to win the hearts and minds of men with pomp and ceremony, with gemstones, silk and cloth of gold, not with a programme of plainness and austerity, which was the path chosen by North European Protestantism. The Gesù was built in 1568–75 to a design by Giacomo della Porta (façade) and his teacher Vignola (interior). The exterior, with its pedimented main elevation and lateral volutes (scrolls), and the interior, with its dizzyingly rich decoration, came to be the model for all Jesuit churches. The ceiling fresco of the *Triumph of the Name of Jesus* is a masterpiece of *trompe l'oeil*: it shows the Jesuit monogram IHS (*Iesus Hominum Salvator*; Jesus Saviour of Mankind), filling the heavens with a bright phosphorescent glow. An angled mirror allows you to examine it without cricking your neck.

The north transept is filled with the great altarpiece-tomb of Ignatius Loyola, founder of the Jesuit Order. Born into a wealthy family in the Spanish Basque Country, Ignatius began life as a proud and swaggering sort of fellow, trained as a soldier and with little time for spiritual contemplation. A battle wound shattered one of his legs, leaving him permanently lame. During his long convalescence, his mind turned to higher things and he rose from his sickbed to spend the rest of his life in the service of God and the Church. His *Spiritual Exercises* are a classic mystical text on union with God, containing prayers and meditations on the life of Christ designed to make the reader more Christ-like. He died in 1556, aged 65, of the Roman fever, in a room in the seminary next door to this church.

In the centre of his altar-tomb, the Jesuit motto, *Ad maiorem Dei gloriam* ('To the greater glory of God'), is picked out in lapis lazuli and gilt. The scenes from St Ignatius's life in high relief are especially vivid, particularly the one that shows him standing at the top of a flight of steps, exorcising demons. The statue group to the right of the tomb is a *tour de force* by the Paris-born sculptor Pierre Le Gros the Younger. It shows Faith confounding Heresy and Hatred: the two malefactors tumble in confusion at Faith's feet while a gleeful little cherub pulls their heretical books to pieces. Anti-Protestant zeal today is not what it once was and the name 'Luther' on the spine of one of the books is tactfully obscured with wax.

Opposite this tomb is the Chapel of St Francis Xavier, companion and follower of St Ignatius, who preached the gospel in Goa, where he is buried. One arm was detached from his body in 1614 and is now preserved here.

Beside the church façade to the right is the entrance to the rooms occupied by St Ignatius and used as his head-quarters from 1544 until his death (*Piazza del Gesù 45; open Mon–Sat 4–6, holidays 10–12*).

San Lorenzo in Damaso
Map p. 302, B2. Open 7.30–12 & 4.30–8.
Housed inside the Renaissance Palazzo della Cancelleria, the Papal Chancery, this basilica is one of the earliest foundations in central Rome. The original church, dedicated to St Lawrence, was built by Pope Damasus I (hence the name, 'in Damaso') in the fourth century. Today's church retains no trace of the original, and is in fact not completely on the same site. It is arranged on a basilica plan, with a very wide nave, and is richly adorned with funerary monuments, including an admonitory and memorable winged skeleton on the west wall, which bears the name of Alessandro Vetrino, trusted chamberlain of Pope Urban VIII. In the south aisle is the tomb of the demure, ringleted Maria Gabriella, wife of rare virtue, laid to rest with her infant son. She was twenty-six.

POPE DAMASUS I

The Roman-born Pope Damasus I (reigned 366–84) was a complex man. In an age when Roman pontiffs were also heads of state, he was efficiently ruthless. In an age also when Rome was tussling for spiritual supremacy with Byzantium, he showed himself to be a canny propagandiser; and in an age when rival claims to the Chair of St Peter were the norm, he was dogged in the pursuit of his own interests, permitting himself to ignore the sixth commandment: thou shalt not kill. He was keen to demonstrate the glorious role his city had played in the triumph of Christianity and did much to preserve the memory and the cults of the Roman Christians who had died for their faith. It was during the reign of Pope Damasus, in 380, that the emperor Theodosius I espoused the Nicene Creed, establishing the orthodoxy of the Roman and Constantinopolitan churches and officially condemning Arianism as a heresy. While Arianism denied the full divinity of Christ, the Nicene Creed describes Him as 'being of one substance with the Father'. Pope Damasus set out with vigour to extirpate Arianism and other heresies. He was also a champion of the authority of Rome: significantly he stopped using the Greek liturgy and translated the language of divine worship into Latin. It was Damasus who set St Jerome the task of compiling a single standard Latin translation of the Bible, the Vulgate (from which the quotation that heads this chapter is taken). He also did much to embellish the tombs of Roman martyrs, adorning many of them with stone plaques carved with laudatory verses of his own composition (*see pp. 112 and 163*). He chose as his burial site the catacombs of Sts Mark and Marcellian (close to those of St Calixtus and Domitilla; *no public access*).

San Lorenzo in Lucina

Map p. 302, C1. Open 8–8.

This lovely church, facing a busy and lively square just off the Corso, was built in the fifth century on the site of an earlier building said to have been the *titulus* of a matron named Lucina, in whose house a community of Christians would meet. Excavations underneath the present building (*only open on the first Saturday of the month at 5pm*) have revealed a hall that perhaps served as the original meeting house. Part of the *Horologium Augusti* also lies under here: this was a great sundial laid out by Augustus to celebrate his conquest of Egypt. Its gnomon was the obelisk that now stands in Piazza Montecitorio.

The first south chapel has a casket under the altar, in which is preserved a part of the gridiron on which St Lawrence, a deacon of the early Church, is said to have been roasted alive in 258, hence the old Latin name for this church, Sanctus Laurentius in Craticula (*graticola* is the modern Italian for a griddle). The early eighteenth-century painting above the altar shows Lucina presenting the ground-plan of the church to St Lawrence, who floats above her on a grey cloud, his gridiron in his right hand and a palm of martyrdom in his left.

Also in the south aisle, beyond the monument to Poussin (*see pp. 208–09*), is the Chapel of the Annunciation, designed by Bernini for the wealthy Portuguese doctor Gabriele Fonseca, personal physician to Pope Innocent X. Like many Bernini chapels, it makes use of natural light: here it is filtered through a lantern to illuminate a coffered ceiling writhing with cherubs and angel musicians. The theme is echoed in the oval altarpiece below, where painted cherubs dance in an aerial circle above the Annunciate Virgin. On the left, the further bust, with its elegant waxed moustache, is Fonseca (d. 1668), leaning from the wall, hand to bosom, in an attitude of supplication.

The high altarpiece is a very expressive *Crucifixion* by Guido Reni, an artist from Bologna who came to Rome with his fellow Bolognese Annibale Carracci, and who found favour with Pope Paul V and his family (the Borghese). In the nineteenth century Reni was a more celebrated artist than Caravaggio and visitors to Rome would come on secular pilgrimage to view his works. Today he is less sought-after, but this altarpiece shows him at his best. The heavens are dark with the threatening storm, the horizon glimmers with an eerie light and Christ's pale body hangs luminously on the Cross.

Santa Maria in Aracoeli

Map p. 302, C3. Open 9–12.30 & 2.30–5.30.

The main west door is approached up a wide and steep flight of steps. The austere façade does not prepare you for the beauty of the interior, with its lovely Cosmatesque floor and its many worn tombstones of knights, ladies and clerics. The first south chapel has beautiful fifteenth-century frescoes by Pinturicchio of the life of St Bernardino of Siena. Set on end in the west wall is Donatello's very worn tombstone of the archdeacon Giovanni Crivelli (1432), with superbly foreshortened feet.

The church stands on the highest point of the Capitoline Hill, on a spot where, according to legend, the emperor Augustus had a vision of Christ. Alarmed at the Roman people's desire to worship him as a god, he had gone to the Tiburtine Sibyl (Sibyl of Tivoli) for advice. The twelfth-century pilgrim's handbook *Mirabilia Urbis Romae* takes up the story:

> [The Sibyl] begged for three days space, in the which she kept a straight fast; and thus made answer to him after the third day: These things, sir emperor, shall surely come to pass:
>
> Token of doom: the earth shall drip with sweat;
> From Heaven shall come the King for evermore,
> And present in the flesh shall judge the world.
>
> And anon, whiles Octavian diligently hearkened unto the Sibyl, the heaven was opened, and a great

brightness lightened upon him; and he saw in heaven a virgin, passing fair, standing upon an altar, and holding a man-child in her arms, whereof he marvelled exceedingly; and he heard a voice from heaven, saying, This is the altar of the Son of God. The emperor straightway fell to the ground, and worshipped the Christ that should come.

It is unlikely that Augustus felt any real dismay at the idea of being worshipped as a god. He had instigated the imperial cult with his deification of Julius Caesar. In time, Augustus became for pagan Romans what Jesus was for Roman Christians: he *was* the everlasting king. His advent had been foretold not by the Tiburtine Sibyl but by the Sibyl of Cumae. Peace, she had prophesied, would spread over the land with the coming of the Son of God. Virgil, the great Augustan propaganda poet, sang in his Fourth Eclogue of a new dawn when a 'boy's birth' would usher in an age of ease and bliss, when sheep need not fear the lion, when man would no longer toil and when the earth would be equally fruitful in all its parts. Stories began to circulate that Augustus was in fact the son of Apollo, who had visited his mortal mother in the guise of a serpent. When Augustus' body was cremated, a senator claimed to see the emperor's spirit ascending to heaven through the smoke. The imperial cult of apotheosised rulers, by which emperors joined the pantheon of the gods after death, was established.

In the north transept, a small temple-like structure stands over a Cosmatesque altar which depicts Augustus and his vision of the Virgin, with the Agnus Dei between them. The large tomb-chest contains relics of St Helen, the mother of Constantine. The relics were moved here in the twelfth century from her mausoleum on Via Labicana (Via Casilina; *map p. 9*) and her porphyry sarcophagus was reused for the burial of Pope Anastasius IV. The sarcophagus is now in the Vatican Museums.

The Cappella del Santissimo Bambino, at the back of the church, preserves a replica of a famous statuette of the infant Christ, decked in jewels. The original was made by a Franciscan friar in the fifteenth century, from

olive wood from the Garden of Gethsemane. It used to be taken to the bedsides of the sick, until it was stolen in 1994 and never recovered. The replica is still much venerated. Holy oil from its lamp is available (free of charge) in the souvenir shop.

Mid-twentieth-century prayer card from the Cappella del Santissimo Bambino, showing the stolen statue. There is a text on the back that reads: 'Most lovable Lord Jesus, may we ever seek Thy greater glory here below so that one day we may come to enjoy Thy infinite beauty in Heaven.'

Santa Maria sopra Minerva
Map p. 302, C2. Open 7–7.

It is interesting how styles of art seem to localise. At the east end of the Dominican church of Santa Maria sopra Minerva, in a corridor to the left of the high altar, is the pavement tomb of Fra' Angelico (d.1455), shown in his monk's cowled habit, hands crossed on his stomach. In a further corridor leading to the sacristy, there are more such effigies, the tomb slabs of monks and clerics, removed from the floor and now upended in the wall, their faces worn, their hands clasped upon their abdomens. Beneath the high altar, between Michelangelo's feeble *Risen Christ* and a nineteenth-century *John the Baptist*, lies St Catherine of Siena, the great Dominican tertiary, youngest of the twenty-five children of a Tuscan dyer, who rose to become co-patron of Rome, Italy and Europe, and who lived here, in rooms just off the sacristy, and died there in 1380 at the age of thirty-three. Her serene effigy (1430) is carved seemingly as a forerunner of all the others in this church, hands on stomach, and it is, in fact, attributed to the same artist as the Fra' Angelico tomb, Isaia da Pisa. She lies a little turned towards the viewer, so one foot has been sculpted longer than the other.

San Pancrazio
Map p. 9. Open 9–12 & 4.30–7, Sun 8–1 & 4.30–8.

The basilica of San Pancrazio is remote from the centre of Rome, on the far side of the Janiculum Hill, beside the ancient Via Aurelia, which led north to Transalpine Gaul along the Tyrrhenian coast. It is a lengthy and slightly arduous, unpleasant walk to get to San Pancrazio, and one feels a sense of inordinate triumph when one finally arrives and sees the plain, windowless façade. It looks an inauspicious spot and the old church is sadly dilapidated. But it has a charm and a story. It was Pope Symmachus who built the first church here, a building which was greatly enlarged and embellished by Pope Honorius I in 630, as part of his programme to erect basilica churches over the sites of prominent martyrdoms or burials (Sant'Agnese fuori le Mura and Santi Vincenzo e Anastasio at Tre Fontane are two of his other accomplishments).

San Pancrazio (St Pancras) was an early fourth-century boy martyr, said to have been beheaded here for refusing to renounce his faith. His body, allegedly abandoned by the roadside, was gathered up by a pious Christian lady and given honourable burial in the nearby cemetery, now the catacombs under the church (*closed for restoration at the time of going to press*).

In decorating the church interior, someone has gone mad with *trompe l'oeil*: not only the side altars but even the pulpits are optical illusions. The effect is amusing but in fact covers a tale of repeated despoliations. The basilica once boasted two fine Cosmatesque ambones (reading desks), destroyed by Napoleonic troops. Then in 1849, during the battle between the Papal States and the armies of Garibaldi, the bones of St Pancras were scattered to the winds, never to be reassembled. All that remains is the head, in a reliquary casket in the south aisle, said to stand over the precise spot where the fourteen-year-old martyr was decapitated.

Santa Prassede

Map p. 303, E2–F2. Open 7–12 & 4–6.30.

Pope Paschal I, Roman-born, was abbot of a monastery near St Peter's before he became pope, and was placed in charge of looking after pilgrims. On his death he chose to be buried in Trastevere. He founded three churches in Rome, and in each of them he left splendid mosaics. Santa Maria in Domnica is one of his foundations (*see p. 129*); Santa Cecilia is another (*see p. 144*); and this, his third, has the finest mosaics of all.

On your left as you enter the church (the entrance is a small door in the south side) is the chapel known as the Chapel of St Zeno, officially dedicated to the Blessed Virgin, implored to deliver us from the torments of hell. Built by Pope Paschal as a mausoleum for his mother, Theodora, it is entirely encrusted in mosaics. Around the entrance door, on the exterior, is a double row of roundels of saints and apostles, with Christ at the summit, flanked by St Paul (dark hair and pointed beard) and St Peter (grey hair and square jaw).

There is a coin-operated light, which is essential for viewing the mosaics in the interior. These show a mixture of saints alive and dead. The square halo denotes

those still living when the chapel was made. The glory of the chapel is its vault: slender angels clad in white, with turquoise haloes, are shown bearing aloft the likeness of Christ in a roundel. Pagan iconography has a long reach: the *topos* of the victorious warrior borne aloft on his shield by winged Nike figures has here transmogrified into Christ the victor over death, borne aloft by heavenly messengers. On the entrance wall are St Peter and St Paul upholding the throne of God. Opposite the entrance are the Virgin and Child flanked by St Praxedes and St Pudentiana, two holy sisters, by tradition the daughters of the senator Pudens, who was converted by St Peter. It is to Praxedes that this church is dedicated (*for the church of Pudentiana, see p. 16*). On the left are St Praxedes, St Pudentiana and other female saints, including Paschal's mother Theodora. On the right: St John the Evangelist, St Andrew, St James, Christ, Pope Paschal and (possibly) St Valentine. Beyond this, in a casket, is one of those stumps of column that often crop up in Roman churches, laying claims to peculiar sanctity. This one makes a particularly audacious one: it purports to be the column at which Christ was flagellated.

There are also very fine mosaics in the apse and on the triumphal arch, with two monograms of Paschal: in every church he founded, Pope Paschal left this 'signature' (*see illustration above*). In the apse, Christ is flanked by Sts

Peter, Paul and Zeno (right) and Praxedes and Paschal (left). The triumphal arch shows the Lamb of God, the seven candlesticks, the symbols of the Evangelists and the twenty-four elders casting down their crowns. The whole decorative scheme is based on the text of Revelation 4:

…and round about the throne were four and twenty seats: and upon the seats I saw four and twenty elders sitting, clothed in white raiment; and they had on their heads crowns of gold. And out of the throne proceeded lightnings and thunderings and voices: and there were seven lamps of fire burning before the throne, which are the seven Spirits of God. And before the throne there was a sea of glass like unto crystal: and in the midst of the throne, and round about the throne, were four beasts full of eyes before and behind. And the first beast was like a lion, and the second beast like a calf, and the third beast had a face as a man, and the fourth beast was like a flying eagle. And the four beasts had each of them six wings about him; and they were full of eyes within: and they rest not day and night, saying, Holy, holy, holy, Lord God Almighty, which was, and is, and is to come. And when those beasts give glory and honour and thanks to him that sat on the throne, who liveth for ever and ever, the four and twenty elders fall down before him that sat on the throne, and worship him that liveth for ever and ever, and cast their crowns before the throne, saying, 'Thou art worthy, O Lord, to receive glory and honour and power: for thou hast created all things, and for thy pleasure they are and were created.'

Steps lead down under the high altar to a tiny, narrow crypt with sarcophagi and a battered Cosmatesque altar. One of the tomb chests, simple, strigilated, with no sculptural decoration, is labelled: 'The body of St Praxedes, the body of St Pudentiana'. The walls are covered with scribbled graffiti, most of it the petitions of the faithful or expressions of thanksgiving from those who have found solace here.

San Silvestro in Capite

Map p. 302, C1. Open 7–12.30.

San Silvestro is an eighth-century foundation, built on the ruins of an earlier building, tentatively identified as the Temple of the Sun built by the third-century emperor Aurelian. The sun cult had found favour with Constantine too, before his conversion to Christianity. This church was built expressly to house the remains of martyrs translated here from the catacombs. Its dedication refers to the relic of the head (*capite*) of St John the Baptist, which is kept in a separate chapel to the left of the main entrance. Since 1885 the church has been administered by the Pallottines, priests and brothers of the Irish Province of the Society of the Catholic Apostolate. Mass can be heard here in English (*see p. 257*).

Santa Susanna

Map p. 303, E1. Open 9.30–11.15 & 4–5.30.

This is the church of American Catholics in Rome and Mass can be heard in English here (*see p. 257*). The façade is by Carlo Maderno, begun in 1597. Though Maderno more famously also designed the façade of St Peter's, it is Santa Susanna that is considered his masterpiece: to appreciate his achievement, its harmonious combination of retreating and projecting volumes and horizontal and vertical lines, you need to approach from Via Torino.

An early Christian *titulus* stood here. In the sixth century it was dedicated (by Pope Gregory the Great) to the

third-century Roman martyr Susanna, who, according
to her legend, was beheaded under Diocletian (note the
emblematic little severed head carved in the pediment
above the entrance door). The decoration in the interior
includes frescoes in the form of *trompe l'oeil* tapestries
slung between *trompe l'oeil* Solomonic columns (very well
done) showing the story of Susanna's biblical namesake,
the Susanna who appears in the book of Daniel, spied on
by the lecherous Elders as she bathes and then embroiled
by them in a blackmail attempt upon her virtue.

In the sacristy on the north side (*ring the tiny red bell;
open 9.30–11.30 & 4–5.45*), under a section of glass floor,
you can see remains of black and white mosaic paving
and a long, narrow sarcophagus. This was found to contain fragments of wall-painting of the eighth century,
which when pieced together revealed St John the Baptist
and St John the Evangelist pointing to a central Lamb of
God; and the Virgin and Child flanked by two female
saints, St Agatha (named) on the left and a figure thought
to be St Susanna on the right. All three women are richly
clad and bejewelled.

The church claims relics of four other saints: St Gen-
esius, a comic actor in rollicking farces that poked fun
at Christianity, who underwent conversion and was beheaded under Diocletian; St Gabinius, reputedly the father of Susanna, also beheaded under Diocletian; St Fe-
licity, a second-century martyr about whom very little is
known for certain; and Pope Eleutherius.

CHRISTIAN MEETS PAGAN

The great church of Haghia Sophia in Istanbul was consecrated by Constantine's son Constantius and dedicated to Divine Wisdom. Its successor church, built by Justinian, was converted into a mosque in 1453 by Mehmet the Conqueror. It is a secularised museum today, but nevertheless, with its great circular calligraphic plaques bearing the names of Allah, Mohammed and the caliphs of Islam, it still stands as a powerful illustration of the triumph of one faith over another.

In Rome the faith that triumphed was Constantine's faith, and it is still dominant. It made its conquest not by the sword, but by word and deed and by good fortune. It was a process that took centuries. All across the empire, beginning with the eastern provinces, pockets of the faith had existed since the death of Christ and they had always been a thorn in the imperial side. A revealing letter survives from Trajan, addressed to Pliny the Younger, who as the keen young governor of Bithynia-Pontus was asking what was to be done about the Christian menace:

'You have done exactly right in examining the cases separately,' Trajan tells him, 'for no one-size-fits-all rule can be applied. Christians should not be sought out. If they are brought before the law and found guilty, they should be punished, unless they recant their faith and make oblations to our gods, in which case pardon them, regardless of what their past actions may have been. Take no account whatever of anonymous denunciations. They set a very bad precedent and are completely out of step with our times.'

From the qualities of restraint, mercy and justice that Trajan displays in this letter, it is easy to understand why Thomas Aquinas nominated him a 'virtuous pagan'. Trajan considered Christians a nuisance, and when they made too public a show, they were executed. But there was to be no hunting-down or full-scale purge.

Two centuries later, Constantine issued his edict permitting Christians to worship as they chose. But he did not convert to Christianity himself at this stage, nor did he make any attempt to suppress the old state cult. It was only later, under Theodosius I, that Christianity was made the official religion of the empire—but Christians by then were more concerned with rooting out heresy in their own ranks than in eradicating pagan worship. In Rome, Pope Damasus I devoted his staunchest efforts against the Arians, the sect that denied the divinity of Christ.

Towards the end of his reign (he died in 395), Theodosius became more active in banning paganism. He closed down its temples, abolished its priesthoods and its cult of deified emperors, and toppled its monuments. Despite the soaring oratory of the consul Symmachus, Augustus' golden statue of Victory, celebrating Rome's prowess in battle and the defeat of Antony and Cleopatra in 31 BC, was removed from the senate house in the Forum. Paganism was outlawed. When in 410 Rome was sacked by the armies of Alaric the Goth, many attributed the disaster to the gods' retribution. St Augustine wrote his *City of God* in eloquent refutation of this theory.

The last emperor of the West, Romulus Augustulus, was deposed in 476, despite a name which had seemed to adumbrate great things: a new Romulus, a little Augustus. The poor boy was neither. He was fourteen years old and he went willingly. The long era of papal pre-eminence had begun.

It might be thought that with the final eradication of pagan religious practice, the popes would throw their mantle over Rome, taking over and 'Christianising' its grandest buildings as Sultan Mehmet took over Haghia Sophia. But this was not so. The process was only gradual. In fact, two of the most visited places in Rome today, St Peter's basilica and the Roman Forum, might seem to have nothing to do with one another: one so obviously Christian, the other, seemingly, resolutely not. This chapter visits some of those places where the pagan and the Christian jostle each other shoulder to shoulder.

THE MILVIAN BRIDGE & ARCH OF CONSTANTINE

Christianity did not conquer with the sword—and yet it was with the sword that the groundwork was laid, at the Milvian Bridge (*map p. 9; to get there, take tram no. 2 from*

Piazzale Flaminio or bus 53 (weekdays only) from St John Lateran, the Colosseum or Piazza Venezia). Today the place is peaceful: but this not particularly impressive-seeming footbridge over the Tiber was the scene, in late October of the year AD 312, of one of the pivotal battles of Western history, where the forces of Constantine vanquished those of his rival emperor Maxentius.

The bridge today is not very much frequented, except by lovers, who come here to clip a padlock to one of the bars placed at intervals along it as a symbol of everlasting attachment. Beyond the clotted love tokens, over the parapet, you can look down on the Tiber below, watch it burbling swiftly over a shallow cataract, and imagine the clash and clamour of horses and men.

Maxentius championed Rome. He made it his capital—he was the first emperor for a hundred years to do so—and set in motion a train of great building projects aimed at restoring the city to its central position within the empire, not just symbolically but actually. He named his son Romulus and dedicated a temple in the Forum (either to his dead son or to the great eponymous founder of the city). His sister Fausta married his co-ruler, the man whom Shelley ostentatiously called the 'Christian reptile'. Constantine was not so much reptilian as amphibious. He was born a pagan but emerged from the water as a Christian, and so died.

And he was unable to share a throne with Maxentius. The two soon came to blows, and battle lines were drawn

IMP·CAES·FL·CONSTANTINO MAXIMO
P·F·AVGVSTO S·P·Q·R
QVOD INSTINCTV DIVINITATIS MENTIS
MAGNITVDINE CVM EXERCITV SVO
TAM DE TYRANNO QVAM DE OMNI EIVS
FACTIONE VNO TEMPORE IVSTIS
REMPVBLICAM VLTVS EST ARMIS
ARCVM TRIVMPHIS INSIGNEM DICAVIT

To the Imperial Caesar Flavius Constantine, the Great, Pius, Felix,
Augustus: inspired by a divinity and in the greatness of his mind, with
his army and by the just force of arms he delivered the state both
from a tyrant and from all his faction; thus the Senate and the People
of Rome have dedicated this arch in token of these triumphs.

at the Milvian Bridge across the Tiber. In order, as he
hoped, to cut off his adversary's retreat, Maxentius had cut
the bridge before the battle commenced. It was an action
that proved his undoing. With his horses and men he was
forced back into the water and there drowned, yielding
the day to his rival. Constantine built an arch to celebrate
his victory. It is one of the most famous of Rome's surviv-

ing ancient monuments, standing beside the Colosseum (*map p. 303, D3*). On its short west face is the goddess Luna in her two-horse chariot. On the long south face is a scene of the Battle of the Milvian Bridge. The short east face has a roundel of the sun god rising from the ocean and a depiction of Constantine's *adventus* into Rome. On the north face we see Constantine in Rome distributing gifts. The inscription which appears on both the north and south faces (identical on each) contains a famously ambiguous religious reference to a '*divinitas*', a divinity, in the singular. What or who was this god? It is an early and important witness of the slow change from the worship of many deities to the worship of a single, all-powerful one. The process by which this happened is fascinating and can be traced all over Rome in its art and architecture.

A digression on Christian art and iconography

Christians at first did not make use of pagan temples for their own liturgy. As the new faith gained ground, so it also came to take over ancient edifices, but no temple was used until the seventh century. The first pagan building to be converted was the Basilica of Junius Bassus on the Esquiline Hill, remodelled by Pope Simplicius as the church of St Andrew (no longer extant)[11].

---

11   The basilica has yielded some beautiful inlaid panels (on display in Palazzo Massimo; *map p. 303, F1*). Junius Bassus' son, also named Junius Bassus, was a Christian. His magnificent sarcophagus can be seen in the treasury of St Peter's.

But just as Sultan Mehmet was happy to retain the dedication of Haghia Sophia, because wisdom is also an attribute of Allah, so too did the early Christians make use of symbols and ideas which came from the old state cult. In part this was a simple case of cultural habit. This new lord Christ must surely look like an emperor? How else can magnificence and power be portrayed? And thus do we see him, toga-clad, in many an early mosaic. In fact, the earliest public devotional Christian art in Rome has no symbolism that we can recognise as explicitly Christian[12]. The Bacchic scenes in Santa Costanza, the mausoleum for Constantine's elder daughter (*fig. 1*), could perhaps be explained as references to Christ the True Vine. But that is not really what they are; they are good old-fashioned Dionysiac revel. Later, as Christianity ceased to be a minority cult and became the official religion of all Romans, we see ideas and motifs that the population at large would be familiar with adopted for a Christian purpose. It was a way of making the new faith, to which all had to adhere, comprehensible, attractive and acceptable. Santa Prassede has a splendid late example in its Chapel of St Zeno (*fig. 2*). The acanthus whorl is another. It occurs as an all-enveloping Tree of Life in mosaics in St John Lateran, San Clemente and Santa Maria Maggiore.

12 Artworks created for private use or for a funerary context are slightly different. The earliest burial tablets from the catacombs have symbols which derive from Jewish precedents alongside motifs which are unambiguously Christian. A cleaner break between the old world and the new is discernible.

Pagan and Christian iconographies combine and intertwine. 1: The vineyard scene from the mausoleum of Santa Costanza (fourth century) shows putti treading the grapes in Bacchic frenzy: it is completely pagan in character. 2: Mosaic from Santa Prassede (ninth century) showing a roundel of Christ borne aloft by angels. The idea is a Christianisation of the image of the victorious warrior borne on his shield by winged Nike figures. 3: Acanthus whorls decorate the pagan Ara Pacis (first century BC) and appear (4) as symbols of eternal life in the Lateran baptistery (fifth century). Finally (5), a scene that is wholly Christian, its ideas derived purely from the Bible: the Nativity of Christ, from a fourth-century sarcophagus in the Museo Nazionale in Palazzo Massimo.

But look at the relief carving on Augustus' Ara Pacis (*fig. 3 on previous page*), the altar dedicated to the great age of peace that he ushered in. There is no fountain of the four rivers at the base, but the idea is the same, a great writhing mass of tendrils springing from a single root. In Christian art, the familiar acanthus is adopted as a symbol of eternal life.

In the Renaissance, the process went back the other way, as Christians rediscovered the Classical world. The German historian of medieval Rome, Ferdinand Gregorovius, writes the following about the reign of Leo X:

> Paganism oozed through every pore of Catholicism in the form of art and religion, of Platonic philosophy and Ciceronian eloquence...In Roman sepulchral inscriptions God is again Jupiter and heaven again Olympus. The cardinals were called senators, the saints simply gods, and the deifying title of *Divus*, as that of *Optimus Maximus*, is usually bestowed on popes. When Leo ascended the throne, the poet Janus Vitalis announced that Jupiter had again descended from Olympus to Rome, and that Leo Medici as Apollo would cure all the maladies of the time.

In few places is this neo-pagan tendency better illustrated than in Castel Sant'Angelo (*map p. 300, D2*), in the Sala Paolina on the upper floor. Here the lavish decoration, a mixture of stucco and *trompe l'oeil* fresco carried out

in the 1540s, shows scenes that are more classically inspired than Christian. The apartment was decorated for
Pope Paul III, Alessandro Farnese, and the bulk of the
decoration shows scenes from the life of his namesake,
Alexander the Great. As you enter, you are confronted
by a fresco of the Archangel Michael emerging from a
trompe l'oeil niche. But turn around and you will see that
the angel is confronting a companion fresco of Hadrian,
whose mausoleum this was and whose spirit still seems
to haunt it. An inscription under the cornice celebrates
the work that the pontiff undertook to restore the ruinous monument to solidity and elegance. No claims are
made that it was turned into a home for Christian piety. In the corners of the ceiling are mottoes in Greek
and Latin: *Dikis Krinon*, 'Lily of Justice', a play on the lily
emblem of the Farnese family; and *Festina Lente*, 'Make
haste slowly', the watchword of Augustus. Only over the
doors do we see a series of Christian themes in the form
of sepia monochrome roundels with scenes from the life
of St Paul, from whom Alessandro Farnese took his regnal name. The message conveyed most powerfully by this
decorative scheme is not the triumph of Christ's church
over paganism but the triumph of the popes, the new
incarnations of ancient imperial majesty.

In the church of San Lorenzo in Lucina (*map p. 302, C1*) is
a simple, unobtrusive little monument to the French artist Poussin. He died in Rome in 1665 and the monument

was placed in the church by Chateaubriand in 1832, at the height of the Neoclassical age, '*pour la gloire des arts et l'honneur de la France*'. Poussin is most famous as a painter of romanticised classical landscapes. The relief carving on the monument (*illustrated opposite*) shows shepherds in an olive grove grouped around a tomb, trying to make sense of the words inscribed in its surface. It is a direct reference to a famous work by Poussin, now in the Louvre, in which exactly the same scene is shown. Written upon the tomb are the words: *Et in Arcadia Ego*. Death comes to all, even to the carefree creatures of Arcadia. Poussin's shepherds are shown in the act of confronting the demise of their own creator.

THE FORUM & PALATINE HILL

Map p. 303, D3. Open 8.30–sunset. There are two entrances, one on Via dei Fori Imperiali (map p. 303, D3) and the other on Via di San Gregorio (map p. 303, D4). There can be long queues at both, though it is possible to pre-book tickets (T: +39 06 39967700). The ticket also covers admission to the ruins on the Palatine Hill and to the Colosseum. You can make your visits on two successive days. Last tickets 1hr before closing. Exits from the Forum bring you out by the Colosseum or close to the Mamertine Prison.

After the Milvian Bridge and the Arch of Constantine, where the great struggle between the Rome of Capitoline

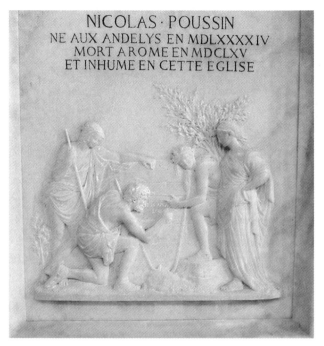

NICOLAS · POUSSIN
NE AUX ANDELYS EN MDLXXXXIV
MORT A ROME EN MDCLXV
ET INHUME EN CETTE EGLISE

'Nicolas Poussin. Born at Les Andelys in 1594, died in Rome in 1665. Buried in this church.' Monument in San Lorenzo in Lucina.

Jupiter and the Rome of St Peter might be said to have begun, one should visit the Forum and the Palatine Hill.

The Christianisation of Rome began from the outside in. St Peter and St Paul were buried and honoured with basilicas well outside the walls; the Aventine and Trastevere were the districts where Christians chose to live; St John Lateran, on the southeastern outskirts, was the first permanent church. Can we expect the Forum to have any Christian traces? It was the heart of pagan Rome, after all.

While it is true that the popes and their flock shunned the Forum during the earliest years, its prime location did not go ignored forever. As the centuries wore on, many of its ruins were built upon and Christianised. If it has no Christian monuments today, we have the archae-ologists to thank for it, who stripped them all away to lay bare the bones of an imperial past. Impatient to dig down to the ancient strata, they did not scruple to remove the temporary veneer of a younger culture. The senate house, for example, the Curia Julia, was converted into a church in 630 but deconsecrated in 1935, when all its Chris-tian fixtures and fittings were removed. The few churches that now remain are either never open (San Lorenzo in Miranda, the former Temple of Antoninus and Faustina) or are entered from outside the Forum (Santi Cosma e Damiano, Santa Maria Nova); the Forum has no life of its own except as an archaeological park, and it is given over to its ghosts. Foremost of these must be Maxentius, who made great efforts to turn Rome into his imperial capital, building a huge basilica on the edge of the Forum. Parts of its vast coffered vaults remain. When Constantine de-feated Maxentius at the Milvian Bridge, he took over the basilica and in its west apse set up a colossal statue of himself, the head and hand and foot of which still sur-vive, in the Capitoline Museums. As you climb from the Forum to the Palatine, you can look back across at the ruined basilica and appreciate the scale of the building, the grandeur to which Maxentius aspired.

The church of Santa Maria Antiqua is the only surviving church in the Forum that is entered from within it. Founded in the mid-sixth century, it was one of the earliest places of Christian worship here and it still exists, albeit ruinous, together with the adjoining Oratory of the Forty Martyrs, home to some interesting wall-paintings.

At the far east end of Forum stands a single-span triumphal arch, the Arch of Titus, erected in AD 81 to celebrate the Roman defeat of the Jewish revolt eleven years previously. The leader of one of the rebel factions, Simon bar Giora, was captured and brought to Rome and paraded in Titus' triumph before being put to death. Among the booty brought to the capital from Jerusalem was the menorah, the seven-branched golden candlestick from the Temple (illustrated on the arch; *see below*).

There have been Jews in Rome since the second century BC: it is the oldest Jewish community in Europe and it furnished for Christianity some of its earliest converts. We know from Suetonius that Claudius expelled the Jews c. AD 49 because of unrest in their ranks 'at the instigation of Chrestus'. It is impossible to know whether this Chrestus was a contumacious Roman Jew (many of their number were Greek-speaking and Chrestus is a plausible name) or whether the reference is to Christ himself, whose message was causing Roman Jews to desert their faith, thus creating disturbances in the community at large.

The Palatine Hill

The Forum can be at once a rewarding place to visit and a frustrating one, laid bare by archaeologists and at the same time made inaccessible by them, with their chains and their Keep Out signs, their messy barricades and slovenly loops of red and white plastic municipal tape, keeping the inquisitive public at bay. The public, probably, were never much welcomed on the Palatine Hill (*map p. 303, D3–D4*). It was here that the emperors had their palace. The popes always eschewed it, sticking to the Lateran and the Vatican. There are two little churches on the east slope of the hill, San Sebastiano and San Bonaventura. Sandwiched between them is a raised walled area called the Vigna Barberini, with the remains of a temple of the Sun and what archaeologists think must have been the revolving dining room of Nero, part of his vast Domus

Aurea, the 'Golden House' which stretched all the way from the Parco Oppio (*map p. 303, E3*) across the Valley of the Colosseum to the Palatine summit. A signboard recreates the view it would have enjoyed, looking out over the huge artificial lake that filled the declivity where the Colosseum now stands. Today, beyond it, the bright white statues on the façade of St John Lateran reach eagerly into the sky.

THE COLOSSEUM

Map p. 303, E3. Opening times as for the Forum; see p. 208.

'You know where is Metro stop?'

The man is thin and he speaks broken English. The tourist he has accosted obligingly tries to help. While she is off her guard, he takes her bag. The police are on the scene within a minute.

'Can you spare me a bit of change for a doss?'

He is also thin, but much better dressed, and his English is perfect. The tourist smiles, shakes her head and walks on.

'Tight bitch!' he shouts after her.

An everyday scene in the Valley of the Colosseum. But this part of central Rome has probably always been like this. The Italian comedians who dress as centurions and pose for photographs for a fee, the Bangladeshis who sell soft drinks, scarves, camera tripods and novelty toys, the

'The Flavian Amphitheatre, noted for its triumphs and spectacles dedicated to the gods of a people of impious cult, redeemed from impure superstition by the blood of martyrs. That the memory of their fortitude may never fade, a memorial was placed on these purified walls by Clement X P.M. in the Holy Year 1675. Destroyed by the dereliction of time, Benedict XIV Pont.M. renewed it in marble in the Holy Year 1750, in the tenth year of his pontificate.'

Romanians who play the violin, the sub-Saharan Africans who spread fake designer handbags on rugs on the cobblestones, so that it's easy to pull up the rug around the merchandise and dissolve into the shadows when the police appear—these people are all the modern incarnations of the touts and huxters, the hustlers and tricksters, and the tradesmen simply trying to earn an honest crust, who have always been drawn to this miasmic spot. Romans, Parthians, Muzirians, Dacians, Nubians, Britons, Gauls; they are all still here.

No building evokes the shudders in quite the same way as the Colosseum. Dungeons do, but differently. This was a place that showcased killing not just as a necessary way of eliminating opponents, nor even as entertainment or a diversion from the daily round like a public hanging, but as an artform.

It is thought that the fight to the death forced upon pairs of men was in origin either an Etruscan or a southern Italian custom, and that it was associated with funeral rites. Staged so lavishly, and before such crowds, however, it became a purely Roman affair. Some members of the audience were appalled by the brutality (Seneca); others clapped with glee and jumped up and down in their seats with delight (Claudius). Close to the Colosseum, below street level between Via di San Giovanni in Laterano and Via Labicana, are the remains of the Ludus Magnus, the largest of the gladiator training schools, where slaves, felons and men captured in battle were taught to fight to please the crowds. Here it was that men learned to kill or be killed. Successful gladiators became heroes, poster boys and sex symbols.

St Peter and St Paul would not have seen the Colosseum. In their day the site was occupied by clustered housing, cleared after the great fire of AD 64 to make way for an artificial lake, part of Nero's lavish Domus Aurea, his Golden House. After Nero's death, the land was returned to the people of Rome in an ostentatious gesture of magnanimity and public-spiritedness by Vespasian, who began this great arena in AD 70. It was completed ten years later, by Vespasian's son Titus, and at its inaugural games, which lasted a hundred days, many thousands of men and beasts spilled their life blood in the sand. The inventive ways in which these deaths were brought about are described by the poet Martial in his *Liber Spectaculorum*, written in honour of the opening games: a criminal nailed upon a cross is transfixed defenceless while his guts are torn out by a bear. A pregnant sow is stabbed with a spear and a living piglet bursts forth. The revolting details are interspersed throughout with fawning praise of Titus. Gladiatorial combat was not outlawed until the fifth century. The last recorded wild beast hunt took place in 523. In the late nineteenth century, when the Colosseum was still a wild and romantic ruin, an English botanist by the name of Richard Deakin produced a catalogue of all the flowers and grasses found growing among its stones. Most were native to Italy but some were very exotic. It is thought that their seeds must have come from the intestines of animals slaughtered here.

The famous tradition that Christians were thrown to the lions in the Colosseum has long been contested, and there are no secure figures of how many met their deaths here and in what circumstances. But whether they were many or few, it was they, with their belief in spiritual equality, who spoke out most forcefully against the games. One cannot condemn a man to fight another man to the death, even if he is only a Gaulish slave. Slave or citizen, he still has an immortal soul. It is, Tertullian tells us in his impassioned denunciation of the games *De Spectaculis*, one of the surest ways that a Christian convert gives his identity away, by his conspicuous absence among the spectators at the arena.

Every year on the evening of Good Friday, the pope leads the candlelit celebration of the Via Crucis at the Colosseum, a symbolic re-enactment, through prayers and readings along fourteen stations, of Christ's journey to Calvary.

THE PANTHEON

Map p. 302, B2. Open Mon–Sat 8.30–7.30, Sun 9–6, holidays 9–1.

There are many examples in Rome of pagan structures now doing service for Christianity. Right in the heart of the ancient city, in the Forum, the church of Santi Cosma e Damiano (*map p. 303, D3*) has been contrived partly from a large hall belonging to the Forum of Vespasian (Forum of Peace). The conversion occurred in the sixth century. Clustered at the foot of the Aventine Hill, around Piazza della Bocca della Verità (*map p. 302, C3–C4*), are a number of churches that occupy older pagan structures. In ancient times this was an area of docks and markets, selling produce and cattle. What may have been a warehouse for the state grain supply became a Christian welfare centre and then, in the eighth century, the church of Santa Maria in Cosmedin. The dockside temples of Hercules Victor and Portunus were converted into churches in the ninth century and later (now deconsecrated). The temples of Juno, Janus and Spes (Hope) became the church of San Nicola in Carcere in the eleventh century.

But there is no more spectacular example of a pagan edifice requisitioned for Christian purposes than the Pantheon. It is spectacular as an extraordinary piece of architectural bravura. And although its dimensions are not well suited to Christian liturgy, it is important because it was the first pagan temple (as opposed to library, grain store or judicial hall) to be reborn as a church.

It was built in the second century, on the site of an earlier building, during the reign of the emperor Hadrian. It takes the form of a pedimented temple porch attached to a domed rotunda: an assemblage of sharp angles meeting a smooth, perfect assemblage of curves. Some have called this juxtaposition amateurish and clumsy, and have cited it as their reason for suggesting Hadrian as architect. Hadrian certainly enjoyed architecture, and he designed a number of buildings. But if the Pantheon was one of them, he did not credit himself. The famous inscription on its external architrave reads: 'Marcus Agrippa, son of Lucius, consul for the third time, made this'. Agrippa had commissioned the earlier temple that stood on this site, and Agrippa remains the person who is honoured.

The Pantheon is dedicated to all the gods. It is a circular temple shadowing the cosmos, built in honour of every divinity in the celestial round. It is a brilliant achievement and most of those who have seen it have not found it clumsy. It has inspired architects from Palladio to Bernini to Thomas Jefferson.

The Pantheon is brilliant not only aesthetically but technically. Though the cylinder of the rotunda has a brick casing, and there are arches of thin bricks inserted into it to act as load-bearing supports, it is built largely out of concrete, a Roman invention, made of crushed stone mixed with volcanic ash. The dome is also of concrete, with deep coffers to lessen the weight. Measuring 43m across, it is the largest unsupported, unreinforced concrete dome ever built. If you view it from outside, you will see that it rises in stepped buttress-rings, added to give support and to counterbalance the dome's own outward thrust, to prevent it from collapsing like an ill-set blancmange.

The effect of that dome, as you enter the Pantheon for the first time, is breathtaking in the deserved sense of the word. Unfortunately it is sometimes difficult to get a full sense of the splendour of this building. It can be oppressively crowded, cluttered with booths selling audio guides, with signs telling you to be silent, with ropes forcing you to go one way and not the other. Everyone reaches for their camera as soon as they get in, holding up the traffic as they do so. The only thing to do is to give yourself time.

The Pantheon was converted into a church in the early seventh century (AD 609) and barrowloads of martyrs' bones were brought here from the catacombs to sanctify it, hence its official name, Santa Maria ad Martyres. The Christian overlay of the surviving pagan structure is detectable but not overpowering. To the ancient bronze entrance doors, roundels have been attached, representing Christ and the Virgin, though from the way she is portrayed, the Mother of God could well be mistaken for a Roman empress on a coin. Inside, on the right, is the imposing, soot-black tomb of Vittorio Emanuele II, first king of the united Italian nation. But no Christian motifs bless his resting place. It is surmounted by a massive eagle within a wreath, identical to the pagan emblem of imperial Rome (*see illustration opposite*). The king is hailed as *Padre della Patria*, 'Father of the Fatherland', a title first accorded to Augustus, as *Pater Patriae*.

Apart from the bones of the martyrs, no saintly or papal relics have found their rest here. There are two kings

(Vittorio Emanuele II and Umberto I), a queen (Margherita, wife of the latter), and a number of artists. It is an Italian hall of fame, and a votive shrine for Italian royalists. Most famous of the artists buried here is Raphael, whose tomb is on the left-hand side. He was so busy being artistically irresistible to popes and cardinals and physically irresistible to artesans' daughters that he failed to marry his virtuous fiancée, Maria. She predeceased him, but is buried here anyway, eternally alongside the man who failed to make a matron of her.

Below: Eagle and wreath from the time of Trajan (d. 117).

Above: Eagle and wreath from the tomb of Vittorio Emanuele II (d. 1878).

The loveliest time to be in the Pantheon is when it rains. You can look up and see the drops falling through the wide ceiling oculus, draining out through the small holes discreetly cut in the marble paving below it. The floor was relaid in the late nineteenth century but its design of squares and circles is the Hadrianic original. Looked at head-on, the squares and circles alternate. Along the oblique axes, each shape runs in a continuous sequence.

THE PROTESTANT CEMETERY

Map p. 301, A3. Open Mon–Sat 9–5, Sun and holidays 9–1. No entry fee, but donations are encouraged and welcomed.

Salus extra ecclesiam non est. There can be no salvation outside the Church. Thus wrote St Augustine in his *De Baptismo contra Donatistas* (c. 400), expressing himself in agreement with his countryman St Cyprian, third-century bishop of Carthage. Later, in 418, he went still further, in his address to the people of the church at Caesarea, saying: 'There can be no salvation except in the Catholic Church. Outside the Catholic Church there can be everything except salvation. A man can hold office, he can partake of sacraments, he can sing "Alleluia" and answer "Amen", he can read the gospel, he can preach in the name of the Father, Son and Holy Ghost. But never, except in the Catholic Church, will he obtain salvation.' Popes down the ages, from Innocent III in the thirteenth century to John Paul II in our own, have broadly concurred: there is no salvation outside the Church.

This 'Church', traditionally, was not an open concept. It was not a belief system of choice such as in our own secularised, *soi-disant* liberal times we might be careful to announce respect for, for fear of seeming intolerant or prescriptive. The early Christians *were* intolerant and prescriptive. They believed that their faith was the only route to salvation. The Second Vatican Council (1962–65) made nods towards an inclusiveness which alarmed traditionalists in suggesting that those who are outside the Church 'through no fault of their own' may perhaps qualify for salvation. But if we stay outside it 'through ignorance, through weakness, through our own deliberate fault,' how much mercy can we expect?

In Rome, Protestants and members of the Greek and Russian Orthodox churches have their own burial ground, familiarly known as the Protestant Cemetery, though more properly it is called the Non-Catholic Cemetery. Until 1870, when the lands of St Peter were conquered for Italy, no non-Catholic could boast on their tombstone of hope for resurrection or eternal life. In this little corner of ground just outside the city walls, on the busy Piazza di Porta San Paolo, the gravestones are revealing. Some are concise, others are prolix, but none of them before 1870 claims that the sleeper will reawaken.

The most prominent burial on this spot is not a Christian of any complexion, but a pagan Roman by the name

Left: Pre-1870 gravestone betraying no hope of a life to come.

Right: Post-1870 gravestone proclaiming the inclusivity of Christ's sacrifice.

of Caius Cestius, who is commemorated by a grey mar-
ble-clad pyramid inscribed in tall letters with his *cursus
honorum* (when viewed from inside the Protestant Cemetery): C · CESTIVS · L · F · POB · EPVLO · PR · TR ·
PL · VII · VIR · EPVLONVM. 'Caius Cestius, son of Lucius, of the *tribus* Poblilia[13], member of the College of the
Epulones, praetor, tribune of the plebs, septemvir of the
Epulones.' The Epulones were a college of priests tasked
with the organising of banquets at official festivals. Cestius died in around 12 BC.

13   The Poblilia or Publilia were a rural tribe (*tribus*) from the Verona area.

The old part of the Protestant Cemetery, a spreading green lawn scattered with memorials to (chiefly British, German and Scandinavian) scholars, artists and grand tourists, contains the grave of Keats, in the far left-hand corner. Keats died in Rome in a house on the Spanish Steps, the victim of a consumption that had eaten away his lungs. He was twenty-five. In his elegy for Keats, *Adonaïs*, Shelley describes the graveyard as 'a slope of green access, where, like an infant's smile over the dead, a light of laughing flowers along the grass is spread...'. His three-year-old son William had been buried here two years previously. Only one year later, Shelley himself would be dead, drowned in a shipwreck off Livorno, and his heart buried here, up at the top of the new part of the cemetery, against its boundary wall. The tragedies of the last years of his life had left a glimmer of belief in some kind of immortality in the proud and outspoken atheist. The poem he addressed to his dead boy reveals it:

Where art thou, my gentle child?
Let me think thy spirit feeds,
With its life intense and mild,
The love of living leaves and weeds
Among these tombs and ruins wild;—
Let me think that through low seeds
Of sweet flowers and sunny grass,
Into their hues and scents may pass
A portion—

OSTIA

Direct trains leave from the Roma–Lido Ostia (Porta San Paolo) station (map p. 301, A3), in the same building as the Piramide Metro stop. Trains are frequent and the journey time is c. 30mins. Get off at the Ostia Antica stop. There is a café-restaurant at the site.

Santa Aurea (grave of St Monica)

When you alight from the train at Ostia Antica, you will do so together with a small huddle of visitors bound for the ruins of the ancient port city. Walk with them across the footbridge from the railway station, and bear them company until you reach the main road of the little town. At this point you leave them: instead of turning left towards the excavations, turn right towards the castle and follow the road as it skirts around its moat. The church of Santa Aurea stands in the little cobbled Piazza della Rocca, a medieval village square with a medieval village atmosphere, surrounded by neat little cottages, supplied with a public drinking fountain, a restaurant in Via del Forno, and a church, all facing the massy protecting flank of the castle itself, built by Giuliano della Rovere, the future Pope Julius II, when he was bishop of Ostia in 1483–1503.

The church is small and very simple, aisleless, with a painted tie-beam ceiling and Stations of the Cross in bold white relief against a vivid blue ground placed high along the walls. In a chapel on the south side, behind glass, is a piece of the tombstone of St Monica, the mother of St Augustine, who died here suddenly in 387, aged fifty-five. Opposite the tombstone there is an Italian transcription of the full epitaph, which translates as follows:

'Here your most chaste mother laid her ashes, Augustine, a further light upon your own merits, you, who as a faithful priest of the holy message of peace instruct by your life your faithful adherents. You are both crowned with immense glory by your works, you and your most virtuous mother, who is made more blessed still by her son.'

St Augustine's own tribute to his mother goes like this:

May she rest in peace with her husband, her only one, after whom she married no other. She served him with patience and obedience, bringing forth fruit unto thee, and at the end won him also for thyself. O Lord my God, inspire thy servants my brethren, thy sons and my masters, whom I serve with voice and heart and pen, that whosoever of them shall read these words, may remember at thy altar Monica thy servant, with Patricius her husband, by whose bodies thou broughtest me into this life, though how it was done I know not. May they remember them in this failing light; they were my parents and also my brother and sister, subject to thee our Father in our Catholic mother the Church, and they will be my fellow citizens in that eternal Jerusalem for which thy people yearn all the days of their pilgrimage.

Confessions Book IX

Behind the high altar, a lamp has been placed upon a slender stump of column, balanced on a pretty fluted stand. These are certainly spolia from Ostia Antica itself.

Ostia Antica (the excavations)

The port city of Ostia, at the mouth of the River Tiber, reached the height of its prosperity in the second century, during the reign of Hadrian. It stood at a point where the river described a great loop, just before debouching into the sea. On the outer curve of this loop were salt marshes and an expansive lake. The medieval town and its castle, built to defend the river mouth, stood on the lakeshore. Today the landscape has changed because the Tiber suddenly altered its course, after a flood in 1557. The loop in the river has disappeared and the salt marshes and lake are no more.

Even by Augustine's day Ostia was no longer the important commercial centre of some 50,000 inhabitants that it had been under Hadrian. The river mouth had silted up and the main port had been moved to a site further north. But Ostia still had fine private homes and public buildings. It was also the seat of a bishopric, and had been since 313, the same year that Constantine granted freedom of worship to Christians. It possessed a small basilica-church on the *decumanus maximus* (the main east–west street), among whose ruins, on a slender architrave supported by Ionic columns, there is the following crudely-inscribed text in abbreviated Latin: IN XP GEP. FISON. TIGRES. EVFRATA. CRIANORVM DVMITE FONTES (In Christ, Geon, Phison, Tigris, Euphrates. Draw near to the fountainheads of the Christians). These are the four rivers mentioned in the second chapter of Genesis, so often depicted in early mosaics, with deer slaking their thirst at their waters. The architrave probably marked the entrance to the baptistery.

Christian motifs can be found scattered over the site. St Aurea, to whom the little church in medieval Ostia is dedicated (*see above*), is said to have been martyred right beside the theatre. And not only Christianity flourished here. Ostia was also a great centre of Mithraism (*see p. 140*) and of other imported cults from Egypt and further east. At the far end of the *decumanus maximus* stand the remains of the synagogue, the oldest in Europe, dating back to the first century. When it was built it would have

The town of Ostia in its heyday was home to numerous cults, which throve alongside the official state religion of ancient Rome. By the seashore stood the synagogue, where the mosaic of the Solomon's Knot shown above is to be found. The raven mosaic is from one of Ostia's many Mithraea, temples of the mystery cult of the sun and fertility god Mithras, who was worshipped exclusively by men. The cult of the Bona Dea, worshipped exclusively by women, was also present at Ostia, as were the cults of Cybele, Serapis and Isis. Christianity flourished too, as revealed by the mosaic of the chalice and fish.

been right beside the sea, but the shoreline has retreated some four kilometres since then.

The ruins of Ostia, somnolently basking under tall umbrella pines, are extremely evocative, a splendid place to while away a whole day. As you make your way along the grass-grown basalt slabs of the *decumanus*, you can easily imagine St Augustine and his mother walking out to the shore through the Porta Marina, past the synagogue, to inquire about their boat to North Africa. We do not know exactly where they were staying, but we know that it was a house with a courtyard garden and there are plenty of surviving brick-built ruins that might have been it, some of them even with traces of an upper-floor balcony. In his *Confessions*, Augustine describes standing at a window with his mother, leaning out and chatting, speculating about the nature of the life beyond. Together they share a brief mystic moment when they seem to touch Eternal Wisdom. Two weeks later Monica was dead, of a sudden fever. Though her initial wish had been to be buried beside her husband, she maintained at the end that she had no fear of dying in a foreign land, for God would surely know where to find her when the Day of Judgement came. Very touchingly Augustine describes how he comes to terms with his grief, examining why he feels so bereft at the death of one who wished to leave this world and who has not, in any real sense, died. Psalm 101 was read over Monica's body:

> My song shall be of mercy and judgement:
>   unto thee, O Lord, will I sing.
> O let me have understanding in the way of
>   godliness.

Augustine returned from his mother's graveside and went to the baths. We cannot know which baths those were; there are several that survive among the ruins of Ostia. Bathing did not soothe him. He retired to bed, wept freely, recited a hymn of St Ambrose (his mentor in Milan) and found himself much comforted.

THE VATICAN CITY, MUSEUMS & SISTINE CHAPEL

Among the many titles held by the pope can be found the following:

Bishop of Rome
Vicar of Jesus Christ
Successor of the Prince of the Apostles
Supreme pontiff of the universal church
Primate of Italy
Archbishop and metropolitan of the province of Rome
Sovereign of the Vatican City State
Servant of the servants of God.

The pope has always been the spiritual leader of the Church of Rome, but historically he was a temporal monarch as well, ruler of all the lands of St Peter, otherwise known as the Papal States, which stretched across Italy from Rome to Ancona. That temporal sway no longer exists and has not done so since 1870, when Italian troops captured Rome and made it the capital of a newly united Italy. But the pope still has the Vatican. Within that tiny fiefdom of less than half a square kilometre, he is an autocratic monarch. He is, as the penultimate title in the above list says, sovereign of the Vatican City State.

Side door of St John Lateran with an inscription of Sixtus V. The title 'Pontifex Maximus' (supreme pontiff or bridge-builder) was a rank originally held by the chief high priest of ancient Rome. From the time of Augustus it was assumed by the emperor and later (perhaps from the reign of Damasus I) came to be adopted by the popes.

It was Pope Pius IX who surrendered to the Italian forces. He retreated to the Vatican and there he and his successors remained until 1929, when a treaty was signed with Mussolini. The broad, straight road that leads into St Peter's Square, Via della Conciliazione, is named after that 'conciliatory' pact. It granted 'extraterritorial' status to St John Lateran, Santa Maria Maggiore, San Paolo fuori le Mura, to the pope's summer palace at Castel Gandolfo outside Rome and, also outside Rome, to the site at Santa Maria di Galeria where the transmitters of Vatican Radio are located.

As well as the radio station, the Vatican has its own independent postal service, newspaper and police force (partly made up of the famous Swiss Guard). It also had its own currency until 2002, when it adopted the euro. Look out for the Vatican euro coins, which have different designs from the Italian ones.

VISITING THE VATICAN

Though the Vatican is a separate state, there are no border controls and the parts of it open to the public can be entered and exited freely. The Swiss Guard patrol the entrances to the palace itself and to the pontifical offices. The guardsmen are friendly and ever willing to pose for photographs. Without a prior appointment, you can visit Castel Sant'Angelo, St Peter's and the Vatican Museums. To see the Vatican Gardens and other parts of the Vatican City, a guided tour must be booked (*see below*).

Tours of the Vatican Gardens
Tours last approx. 2hrs and are offered daily except Wed and Sun. For up-to-date information, see the Vatican website, www.vatican.va, and click on 'Vatican Museums' and then 'Guided Tours'. Email address: visiteguidategruppi.musei@ scv.va (to organise a group tour); visiteguidatesingoli.musei@ scv.va (for individual tours). T: (+39) 06 69883145 or (+39) 06 69884676.

Papal audiences

Audiences are held on Wednesdays, either in the Audience Hall or, if weather permits, in St Peter's Square. Tickets are free, but must be applied for in advance and in writing (you can download and print out the request form) by fax or post (no email). Address your request to: The Prefecture of the Papal Household, 00120 Vatican City State; Fax: (+39) 06 6988 5863. To apply in person, go to the Portone di Bronzo under the right-hand colonnade in front of St Peter's (8–10.30 & 3–7.30). For up-to-date information, see the Vatican website, www.vatican.va (click on 'Prefecture of the Papal Household').

CASTEL SANT'ANGELO

Map p. 302, A1 and p. 300, D2. Open Tues–Sun 9–6.30. Café. This circular fortress began life as the mausoleum of the emperor Hadrian. Completed in AD 139, it was the final resting place of Hadrian himself and of a number of his successors. Later it became the papal treasury and a stronghold in times of danger, linked to the Vatican Palace by the famous Passetto or Corridoio, a covered passageway that runs along the top of the Vatican City's defensive wall. During the siege of Rome in 1527, when the armies of the Holy Roman Emperor sacked the city, Pope Clement VII fled to Castel Sant'Angelo along the Passetto. The castle was defended by loyal troops, among whom was the goldsmith Benvenuto Cellini. He writes boastfully of the incident in his autobiography.

Highlights of Castel Sant'Angelo include: the inner access corridor, which winds around inside the building to the sepulchral chamber where Hadrian's sarcophagus once lay; the lift shaft said to have been built to hoist the corpulent Leo X to the papal apartments on the upper floor; the papal apartments themselves, some of them beautifully decorated and which include Clement VII's bathroom; and the ramparts.

The name Castel Sant'Angelo derives from the story of the vision of Pope Gregory the Great, who was crossing the Tiber during an outbreak of plague when he saw an apparition of the archangel Michael on top of the castle, in the act of sheathing his sword. The act heralded an end to the epidemic, and in gratitude a bronze statue of the angel was placed on the summit of the fortress.

For St Peter's Basilica, see p. 70.

THE VATICAN MUSEUMS & SISTINE CHAPEL

Open Mon–Sat 9–6, last entry at 4pm. Entrance on Viale Vaticano; map p. 300, B1. Metro A to Ottaviano, or walk from St Peter's Square. The museums are closed on major Christian festivals and on some other days, sometimes at short notice. For a calendar, see www.vatican.va (click on 'Vatican Museums'). You can book tickets online to avoid having to queue at the entrance.

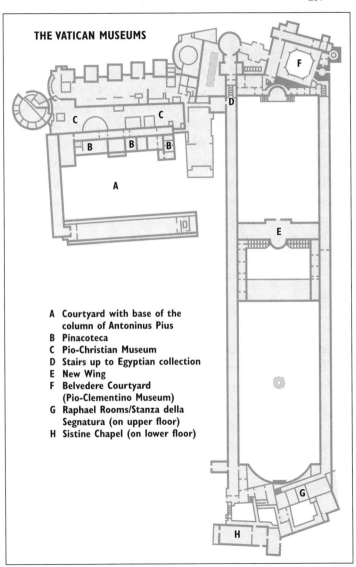

THE VATICAN MUSEUMS

A Courtyard with base of the
  column of Antoninus Pius
B Pinacoteca
C Pio-Christian Museum
D Stairs up to Egyptian collection
E New Wing
F Belvedere Courtyard
  (Pio-Clementino Museum)
G Raphael Rooms/Stanza della
  Segnatura (on upper floor)
H Sistine Chapel (on lower floor)

It was only in the late fourteenth century that the popes began to use the Vatican as their headquarters. Before that they had resided in the Lateran Palace, attached to the earliest of all the churches of Rome, St John Lateran, which is still the cathedral of the city. When the pope and his curia returned to Rome in 1377, after almost seventy years in Avignon, they found the Lateran Palace uninhabitable and chose instead to base themselves in the old papal guest house next to St Peter's. Over the centuries, this house was enlarged and embellished; gardens stretching over forty-four hectares were laid out around it; and it became the papal complex that it is today, the beating heart of the Vatican City.

Housed within that complex are the Sistine Chapel and the Vatican Museums. The museums are one of the greatest treasure-houses on earth, filled with ancient statuary (including the world-famous *Apollo Belvedere* and *Laocoön*), paintings and frescoes by great masters, Egyptian and Etruscan antiquities, priceless books and manuscripts, papal carriages and automobiles, inscriptions from the catacombs and precious examples of early Christian art. It is difficult to enumerate highlights, as a choice so clearly depends on personal interests and taste. Nevertheless, below are a handful of things which should not be missed.

The Apotheosis of Antoninus Pius
The open courtyard at the top of the entrance escala-

tor or ramp **(A)** takes the form of a raised terrace from
which you can view part of the Vatican Gardens. In this
courtyard has been placed a large block of marble carved
with relief scenes and dating from the mid-second century (*illustrated above*). It is the base of the lost Column
of Antoninus Pius, which stood west of the Corso. The
apotheosis scene shows the deified emperor and his empress, Faustina, holding the sceptres of Jupiter and Juno,
accompanied by two eagles as they are borne heaven-
wards by a winged figure holding a globe and serpent.
The female personification of Rome, dressed in martial
attire, waves farewell.

The ancient Roman apotheosis is not the same as the
Christian resurrection. In this scene we see the deceased
emperor not simply being raised from the dead but in

the act of becoming a god. The Romans conferred divinity on their rulers after death, whereas for Christians the living Jesus *was* the Son of God, divinity clad in human flesh, able to cast out devils and perform miracles. No Roman emperor ever wrought a miracle. Their role was to be victorious in war and to ensure political stability and a constant grain supply.

Pinacoteca

The Vatican Picture Gallery (Pinacoteca; **B**) is small enough to be visited without attendant exhaustion and it contains some exceptional pieces by Giotto, Fra' Angelico, Raphael and Leonardo da Vinci. **Giotto's Stefaneschi Triptych** used to stand on the high altar of the old St Peter's. It takes its name from the cardinal who commissioned it, Jacopo Stefaneschi (*for the story of how Giotto impressed the pope and was first summoned to Rome, see p. 60*). The triptych panels are painted on both sides: one was visible to the congregation and the other to the officiating clergy. On the back (clergy side), the central panel shows St Peter enthroned, with St George presenting Stefaneschi (he offers an image of the altarpiece to St Peter). On the side panels are St James, St Paul, St Andrew and St John the Evangelist. On the front (congregation side), the central panel shows Christ enthroned, surrounded by angels, again with the donor Stefaneschi kneeling. On either side are scenes of the martyrdom of St Paul and the crucifixion of St Peter. The latter shows a landscape similar to that depicted on the bronze basilica door (*illustrated on p. 77*). St Peter's cross stands between an anachronistic Castel Sant'Angelo and a Roman pyramid tomb. The scene of the martyrdom of St Paul also has affinities with the bronze door (*see illustration on p. 39*).

Raphael's *Transfiguration*, hailed by many as the artist's masterpiece, was still incomplete when he died in 1520. It was borne before his coffin, in his funeral procession to the Pantheon. A mosaic copy of the work can be seen in St Peter's (*see plan on p. 78*). It is a typical High Renaissance work, full of human figures, with two conflicting centres of attention: the Transfiguration itself at the top, with the serene and shining Christ appearing in a blaze of silvery light to the befuddled disciples, and the foreground scene, full of frenzied gesticulation, of the healing of a young man possessed by a demon. For anyone sitting in church listening to a lengthy and perhaps not very interesting sermon, it would have provided a diversion and a delight.

Pio Christian Museum

The lapidary fragments in this collection **(C)**, mainly from the catacombs, are a must for anyone interested in the development of Christian iconography and the fascinating way in which it evolved from earlier precedents. Very famous is the full-length **statue of the Good Shepherd** (c. AD 300), showing a young man bearing a lamb upon his shoulders. The identification of Christ as the Good Shepherd is obvious ('I am the good shepherd: the

good shepherd giveth his life for the sheep.' *John 10:11*),
but this statue type is much older than Christianity. It
developed from ancient Greek images of young men taking animals to be sacrificed (the *kriophoros*, for example,
is a statue type showing Hermes bearing a ram across his
shoulders) and from there came to be used as a metaphor
for Christ, both Good Shepherd and sacrificial Lamb.
Because of this continuity and adaptation of ideas (and
there are plenty of other examples of it), it is not always
easy to be sure whether an early work of art is Christian
or pagan. For Christians during the centuries when their
faith was subject to persecution, this ambiguity may have
been all to the good.

The collection is also full of carvings and inscribed
slabs showing crude but charming renderings of familiar
stories from scripture. There is a beautiful third-century
tomb slab showing the Adoration of the Magi, for example. The kings arrive with their chests puffed out in
front, cloaks billowing behind, bearing their gifts before
them. Above them hovers a six-pointed star.

Statues from Hadrian's Villa

Hadrian is one of the most interesting and enigmatic of
all the pagan emperors. He was a man of contrasts, described in the *Historia Augusta* as: 'in the same person austere and genial, dignified and playful, dilatory and quick
to act, niggardly and generous, deceitful and straightfor-
ward, cruel and merciful, and always in all things change-

able.' He was a very cultured man, interested in art and architecture. Unlike his predecessor Trajan, his interest was not in extending the boundaries of his empire but in consolidating what he had, making sure that its borders held firm. But this does not mean he was inward-looking. The Roman civilisation spread peace through uniformity. All over their empire they built semi-identical cities, each with its temples, its baths, its forum, its theatre and amphitheatre, its circus, its mosaics of Dionysus and the Four Seasons, its public latrines. But Hadrian was not a conformist. He was exceptionally well-travelled and he was interested in the diversity of the peoples he ruled. His own architectural designs flouted the rules; they were almost baroque. In fact, the things that Hadrian admired most lay outside Rome, in Greece and Egypt. At his enormous, sprawling villa near Tivoli he created a little microcosm of his empire, with miniature versions of its beauty spots, from Athens to Thessaly to the Nile Delta to Asia Minor. Some of the statuary recovered from his recreation of the canal which linked Alexandria to the city of Canopus is displayed in the Vatican's Egyptian Museum **(D)**.

Hadrian built his Tivoli villa on land that belonged to his wife, the empress Sabina. Their marriage was loveless and childless. It is probable that Hadrian was homosexual. The image of his favourite, the beautiful Bithynian youth Antinoüs, haunts the museums of the world like a flitting ghost, portrayed in many a portrait bust or full-length statue, with drooping head, pouting lips and downcast eyes. Antinoüs died in mysterious circumstances, drowned in the Nile in AD 130, at the age of nineteen. Immediately the disconsolate emperor deified him and founded the city of Antinoöpolis on the river's east bank. Many theories exist about this famous death: few believe that it was an accident. Perhaps the boy was getting beyond the age when it could be seemly for him to belong to Hadrian's entourage. Or perhaps it was a ritual suicide. The cult of Antinoüs continued well beyond Hadrian's day. The early Church fathers were in no two minds about it: Tertullian, Origen, St Athanasius and St Jerome are united in their opinion that Antinoüs was merely a man and that his worship was not worship, but idolatry—though they differ in how they express themselves. For St Athanasius, Antinoüs is a lascivious wretch. For Tertullian he is a hapless victim, a person who perhaps had little choice. From this distance, and with our utterly different social outlook, we can have no true idea. The Vatican Egyptian collection exhibits a statue of Antinoüs in the guise of the god of the underworld, Osiris, reborn from the Nile waters. It is a most extraordinary piece, offering a small, perhaps baffling, glimpse into one of the ways in which people have attempted to make sense of death and immortality.

Chiaramonti Museum

The wide, well-lit part of this museum known as the New Wing (Braccio Nuovo; **E**) is approached down a long corridor lined with the portrait busts of Roman men and women, some famous, some divine, some completely unknown. It is a most impressive display and the skills of portraiture are amazing. Famous works in the Braccio Nuovo include the **Augustus of Prima Porta**, a full-length statue of the emperor addressing his troops; a copy of **Polyclitus' Spear-bearer** or *Doryphoros*; and a **bust of Julius Caesar**. Displayed near the bust are two **gilded bronze peacocks** which once stood outside Hadrian's mausoleum (Castel Sant'Angelo). The peacock was the emblem of Hadrian's family and to the ancients it was an attribute of the goddess Juno, also a symbol of the sun and hence of life itself. In Christian times it was adopted as a symbol of immortality.

Pio-Clementino Museum

The part of the Vatican Palace known as the Belvedere was once just that: a hilltop pavilion in the gardens, commanding fine views. The octagonal, open-air Belvedere Courtyard **(F)** was first filled with ancient sculpture by Pope Julius II, and there are benches here where he, and millions of visitors after him, could and can contemplate the various masterpieces. The best-known are the **Apollo Belvedere** and *Laocoön*. The former is a second-century Roman marble copy of a Greek bronze original. It has been very much admired over the years. Byron adored it and modelled his own haircut on it; Napoleon drooled over it (and stole it; it was returned in 1815); artists have sought to imitate it. Albrecht Dürer copied its stance for the figure of Adam in his 1504 engraving of the Fall (Rijksmuseum, Amsterdam). Ruskin disliked it (of course).

The *Laocoön* (first century BC) illustrates the story of the priest of Apollo at Troy, who warned his fellow Trojans about the trickery of the Greeks and urged them not to bring the wooden horse inside the walls. In anger, Apollo sent giant serpents to crush Laocoön and his sons.

In the final room, displayed opposite one another, are two huge porphyry sarcophagi, the tomb-chests of St Helen, mother of Constantine, and her grand-daughter Constantia. The **sarcophagus of Helen** (d. 330) is quite extraordinary. No reference is made to her famous discovery of the True Cross or indeed to her Christianity. Instead we see a line of mounted Roman cavalrymen cutting down barbarians, with what look uncannily like torpedo shells falling about them. It is thought, in fact, that this tomb-chest had originally been intended for Constantine himself. The mausoleum where it originally stood still partially survives, on Via Casilina, the ancient Via Labicana, at the junction with Via San Marcellino. Though not open, it is visible from the road. It has partially collapsed and the amphorae inserted in the masonry to make it lighter, a common Roman building technique, can clearly be seen.

Constantia's sarcophagus is described on p. 178.

Raphael Rooms

The rooms are four in total **(G)**, decorated by Raphael

and his pupils for popes Julius II, Leo X and Clement VII. Raphael worked on them from the time of his arrival in Rome in 1508 until his death in 1520. The themes are the triumph of the Church and the glorification of the popes. All the works are imbued with the spirit of the Renaissance and their frequent reference to the gods of the pagan pantheon makes some of them seem in themselves pagan. Ruskin found them interesting but did not like them. Writing of the Stanza della Segnatura, the room where the pope would sign letters and bulls and which contains the famous **Parnassus** and **School of Athens**, he wrote: 'And from that spot, and from that hour, the intellect and the art of Italy date their degradation.' For him, in this kind of painting, the stern vitality of the Middle Ages, its quirkiness, originality and charm, give place to the perfection-obsessed Renaissance, when art was all derivative, striving to do again what had been done before in the days of Classical antiquity. 'Of Raphael,' he tells us, 'I found I could make nothing whatever. 'The only thing clearly manifest to me in his compositions was that everybody seemed to be pointing at everybody else, and that nobody, to my notion, was worth pointing at.' The remarks are amusing when you read them in front of his *School of Athens*: all the scientists, mathematicians and philosophers gathered around Plato and Aristotle are gesticulating at each other. There is even more finger-pointing in the fresco opposite, the **Disputation on the Holy Sacrament**.

The Sistine Chapel

The Sistine Chapel **(H)** takes its name from Pope Sixtus IV, who commissioned it in 1475. Its dimensions, taller than it is wide, correspond to those given for Solomon's Temple in the first book of Kings:

> 'And the house which king Solomon built for the Lord, the length thereof was threescore cubits and the breadth thereof twenty cubits and the height thereof thirty cubits.'   *1 Kings 6:2*

This gives a ratio of 1 : ½ : ⅓. The Sistine Chapel's measurements (rounded down) are 40m long by 13m wide by 20m high. It is here that cardinals meet in conclave to elect a new pope. The decoration of the ceiling, painted by Michelangelo, is one of the most famous frescoes in the world. But it should not be viewed in isolation, for the decoration of the chapel as a whole, though executed non-chronologically and some sixty years apart, forms a coherent narrative sequence:

- **The ceiling** depicts the world *ante legem*, before the Law, depicting the Creation, the Fall, the Flood, and the pagan Sibyls and Old Testament prophets who foretold the coming of a Saviour;

- **The right-hand wall** (viewed from the altar) shows the world *sub lege*, under the Old Law of Moses;

THE SISTINE CHAPEL

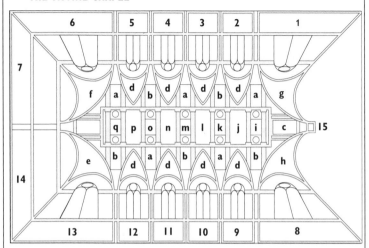

CEILING

a Sibyls
b Prophets
c Jonah
d Forerunners of Christ

Old Testament scenes

e Judith and Holofernes
f David and Goliath
g Punishment of Haman
h Moses and the Serpent of Brass

Scenes from Genesis

i Separation of Light from Darkness
j Creation of Sun and Moon
k Separation of Land from Water
l Creation of Adam
m Creation of Eve
n Expulsion from Paradise
o Sacrifice of Noah
p The Flood
q Drunkenness of Noah

WALLS

Scenes from the life of Moses

1 Circumcision
2 Leading the Israelites out of Egypt
3 Crossing the Red Sea
4 The Tablets of the Law
5 Stoning of Moses
6 Death of Moses
7 St Michael with the body of Moses

Scenes from the life of Christ

8   Baptism
9   Temptation
10 Calling of the Apostles at the Sea of Galilee
11 Sermon on the Mount
12 Entrusting the Keys to St Peter and Stoning
13 Last Supper and Passion of Christ
14 Resurrection

15 Last Judgement

- **The left-hand wall** shows the world *sub gratia*, under the New Law of Christ;

- **The altar wall** shows the Second Coming and Last Judgement, the culmination of all things.

Michelangelo painted the first and last part of this sequence, the ceiling and altar wall, beginning in 1508 and 1536 respectively. The results are justly famous, and to see them is the goal of almost every visitor to Rome. The scenes on the ceiling are explained on the plan on the previous page. The *Last Judgement* shows Christ erupting from the Heavens, one arm raised in condemnation of the wicked, the other outstretched in blessing on the good. Below Christ are St Lawrence and St Bartholomew (the latter's flayed skin bearing a self-portrait of Michelangelo) and below these again the last trumpets sound, unleashing a confused maelstrom of saints, martyrs and the resurrected dead. The virtuous are being pulled to Heaven while demons shovel sinners into the maw of Hell.

The scenes on the side walls were painted in 1481–83 by a variety of masters, including Perugino (Raphael's teacher) and Botticelli. They are very beautiful and often overlooked. Composed in the typical medieval narrative style, with successive episodes occurring within the same frame, they unfold the story of how the Law of God, as revealed to Moses, came to be fulfilled in Christ. The main subjects of each panel are indicated on the plan on the previous page.

The scenes are most interesting if viewed not simply as one sequence going along the right wall (Moses) followed by another going along the left (Christ) but across the chapel as matching and correlative pairs, mirroring and reinforcing each other and continuing each other's message, as it were antiphonally. The first pair, for example, shows the 'old rebirth' by circumcision, that is, acceptance into the community by means of the old custom (Moses' path is shown barred by an angel and then unblocked as his son is circumcised in the bottom right-hand corner); and the 'new rebirth' by baptism. The fourth pair shows Moses receiving the Tablets of the Law (above a scene of the Adoration of the Golden Calf); and the Sermon on the Mount, where Christ says: 'Think not that I am come to destroy the Law: I am come not to destroy but to fulfil.' (*Matthew 5:17–18.*) The fifth pair shows the attempted stoning of both Moses and Christ (in the second case behind the principal scene of the entrusting of the keys to St Peter) and in each panel there is the repeated motif of a triumphal arch.

PRACTICAL INFORMATION

GETTING AROUND

To and from the airport

There are frequent trains linking Fiumicino Airport with Termini Station (journey time 30mins). Ciampino is served by a shuttle bus linking with Metro A. Taxis are plentiful at the ranks outside the airports.

By taxi

Most taxi drivers in Rome are honest, but sadly not all. For the unwary, or those not able to have a full-scale argument in Italian, avoid taking a taxi from outside Termini Station. There are no cruising cabs in Rome (though if you flag down an empty cab, it will stop); normally taxis are picked up from the ranks around town. Convenient ones are located at Piazzale Ostiense, Piazza di Spagna and Piazza del Popolo. Always make sure that the meter is functioning and that you are in a licensed cab: a metal plaque with the driver's name and number will be displayed inside the taxi, typically on one of the rear doors.

By bus

The system of public buses is efficient, though buses can be crowded and services frustratingly infrequent. Signs at bus stops show the routes of each bus line that stops there. Tickets can sometimes be purchased at machines on board, but not always. Since drivers do not sell tickets, it is best to equip yourself beforehand (see section on tickets overleaf).

By Metro

At the time of writing Rome had two Metro lines intersecting at Termini Station and a third one was being built. Few of the stops are in the heart of the city. Useful stops on the two currently functioning lines are as follows:

Line A (red)

Cipro (good for the Vatican Museums)

Ottaviano (good for the Vatican Museums and St Peter's)

Flaminio (at the northern end of the Corso)

Spagna (Spanish Steps)

Repubblica (for Santa Maria Maggiore)

Termini (the central railway station, also good for Santa Maria Maggiore)

Line B (blue)

Colosseo (the Colosseum)

Circo Massimo (Circus Maximus)

Piramide (Piazzale Ostiense, for trains to Ostia)

Basilica S. Paolo (San Paolo fuori le Mura)

Trains are often crowded and covered in graffiti, and stations are gloomy. Nevertheless, for outlying destinations such as the Basilica of San Paolo fuori le Mura, the Metro can be useful.

Tickets on public transport

Tickets should be bought in advance. They are sold at railway stations and at tobacconists. There is a three-day tourist pass available, or else you can buy the so-called BIG (daily pass) or BIT (single-journey ticket). Tickets must be validated at the machines at the entrance to railway and Metro stations, or on board buses or trams. Inspectors carry out random checks.

On foot

For pilgrims, walking is often the preferred way of getting around, and in the centre of Rome it is the best way.

WHERE TO STAY

Rome is not lacking in hotels and guest houses. There are hundreds of them, adapted to all budgets, and ample information is available online. For the pilgrim, a room in one of the numerous convents that offer hospitality is an excellent option. Some of them are extremely central, rooms are basic but comfortable, many have their own bathroom, and not all apply a curfew. For more information, consult Monastery Stays: www.monasterystays.com.

FOOD & DRINK

Rome is filled with restaurants, bars, cafés and snack stands. It is beyond the scope of this book to give listings, but the following few tips might be helpful.

Roman food is simple and good and the ingredients used are mostly fresh and seasonal. Typical dishes include *bucatini all'amatriciana*, pasta served in a sauce of bacon, tomato and pecorino cheese. *Spaghetti carbonara* is also popular as are various types of long pasta with the sauce called *caciopepe* (made with a mild cheese and plenty of freshly ground pepper). Artichokes are plentiful. Zucchini flowers (*fiori di zucca*) are delicious stuffed with mozzarella and anchovies and fried in a light batter. Typical side orders of vegetables include *cicoria* (chicory), steamed and dressed with olive oil; radicchio; and *puntarelle*, sprouting chicory tips, served with an anchovy sauce.

Popular meat dishes include *saltimbocca alla romana* (veal escalope with ham and sage) and *coda alla vaccinara* (stewed oxtail). A very typical dish is *pajata*, the intestines of suckling lamb with the mother's milk still inside them. Not for the faint-hearted. They are served with *rigatoni* (pasta tubes).

Rome is the home of the oldest diaspora community of Jews in the world and their cuisine survives. It can be sampled in a variety of places in the area of the old ghetto, on and around Via del Portico d'Ottavia (*map p. 302, B3–C3*).

Although most of the staples of the Jewish-Roman repertoire were devloped during the ghetto years, from the
mid-sixteenth century, it is just possible that St Paul himself once enjoyed a plate of fried artichokes (*carciofi alla
giudea*).

Romans keep later hours than Americans or northern Eu-
ropeans. Lunch happens at about 1pm and at weekends
or on holidays it can continue long into the afternoon.
Since most churches close in the middle of the day, only
reopening at around 3.30 or 4, a leisurely lunch can be
nicely fitted in to a pilgrim itinerary. In the evenings, restaurants are mainly empty before 8pm.

Getting served in a bar requires a forceful approach.
Don't stand meek and silent: you need to make yourself
heard. There is no etiquette of waiting in line; you have
to assert yourself and if you don't, someone else will step
in ahead of you. If you ask for one of the ready-made
sandwiches, the barman will probably offer to heat it up
for you. It is normal to drink coffee standing up: there is
usually a higher price charged for table service. In many
places you will need to place your order first, pay at the
cash desk and then hand your receipt (*scontrino*) to the
barman to get served.

Service is included in the bill. You do not have to leave a
tip, though a few coins are always appreciated.

CHURCH SERVICES IN ENGLISH

NB: Information about service times was correct at the time of going to press. But it is advisable to check beforehand.

Anglican: All Saints. Sundays at 8.30 (BCP no music) and 10.30 (Sung Eucharist). *Via del Babuino 153. www. allsaintsrome.org. Beyond map p. 302, C1.*

Baptist: Rome Baptist Church. Sundays at 10.30. *Piazza San Lorenzo in Lucina 35. www.romebaptist.org. Map p. 302, C1.*

Catholic: San Silvestro in Capite. Sundays at 10am and 5.30pm. *Piazza di San Silvestro in Capite. www.sansilvestroincapite.com. Map p. 302, C1.* **Santa Susanna**. Saturdays and weekdays at 6pm, Sundays at 9 and 10.30am. *Via XX Settembre. www.santasusanna.org. Map p. 303, E1.* **St Patrick's**. Sundays at 10am. *Via Boncompagni 31, corner of Piemonte. www.stpatricksrome.com. Beyond map p. 303, E1.*

Episcopal: St Paul's Within the Walls. Sundays at 8.30 (BCP) and 10.30. *Via Napoli 58 (corner of Via Nazionale). www.stpaulsrome.it. Map p. 303, E1.*

Methodist: Ponte Sant'Angelo Methodist Church. Sundays at 10.30. *Via del Banco di Santo Spirito 3. www.methodistchurchrome.org. Map p. 302, A1.*

Presbyterian: St Andrew's. Sundays at 11. *Via XX Settembre 7. www.presbyterianchurchrome.org. Map p. 303, E1.*

WALKING TO ROME

The **Confraternity of Pilgrims to Rome** (CPR) has an interesting and informative website, of particular use to those planning to journey to Rome on foot: www.pilgrimstorome.org.uk.

For those planning to follow all or part of the **Via Francigena**, the medieval pilgrims' route across the Alps from northern Europe (the route which Archbishop Sigeric followed), the following website will be useful: www.viafrancigena.com.

APPENDICES

PAPAL INDULGENCES

Miserere mei, Deus: secundum magnam misericordiam tuam. Et secundum multitudinem miserationum tuarum, dele iniquitatem meam.

These are the first two lines of the *Miserere*, Psalm 51, the whole of which was famously set to music by Gregorio Allegri in the reign of Pope Urban VIII (reigned 1623–44) for performance in the Sistine Chapel during Holy Week. If you do not own a recording of it, you can find it easily online[14].

Allegri's *Miserere* is, some would claim, one of the most beautiful pieces of sacred music ever composed. The Vatican cardinals certainly thought so and it is said that they placed it under lock and key, refusing to let a single copy leave their hands, in order to preserve its value and reputation. But it leaked out—according to the popular account, thanks to Mozart, who heard it sung and then wrote it out from memory, an early example of copyright theft. In the beautiful English translation from the King James Bible, the *Miserere* begins like this:

> Have mercy upon me, O God, according to thy lovingkindness; according unto the multitude of thy tender mercies blot out my transgressions. Wash me throughly from mine iniquity, and cleanse me from my sin. For I acknowledge my transgressions: and my sin is ever before me.

14 A particularly recommended rendering is the one by the Tallis Scholars, sung in Merton College Chapel, Oxford, in 1980. At the same time (and on the same CD) they recorded Palestrina's *Missa Papae Marcelli*, composed for the Roman curia in 1555 and dedicated to the late pope Marcellus II, who reigned for twenty-two days and who now lies at rest in a beautiful stone sarcophagus in the crypt under St Peter's.

One of the chief reasons for making a pilgrimage to Rome was—
and for many still is—to gain absolution: to have one's transgres-
sions blotted out. When Pope Boniface VIII proclaimed the first
Holy Year in 1300 (*see p. 74*), he promised pilgrims 'the remission
not only full but also absolute' of all their sins. But how does this
work? What *is* an indulgence?

In the time of Leo X (reigned 1513–21), indulgences acquired a
bad name because they had been turned into a tangible commod-
ity, traded for money like raffle tickets, the proceeds going towards
the building of the great new basilica of St Peter's. The practice so
shocked Martin Luther that he launched a Reformation, framing
an eloquent protest against papal abuses, his famous ninety-five
theses, and nailing them to the church door in Wittenberg. Among
the theses we find the following: 'The pope's wealth today is greater
than the riches of the richest; why does he not build at least this
one church of St Peter's with his own money, rather than with the
money of poor believers?' (Thesis 86) and 'They preach the law
of man who say that as soon as the penny clinks into the money-
box, the soul flies out of purgatory' (Thesis 27). The theses in their
entirety make stirring reading. Luther is in no doubt that 'those
who believe that they can be certain of their salvation because they
have indulgence notes will be eternally damned' (Thesis 32). His
is the great debate between grace and works. Can one really obtain
salvation by special favour rather than by being a good person?
Luther thinks not. 'They who teach that contrition is not necessary on the part of those who intend to buy souls out of purgatory
preach unchristian doctrine,' he tells us. 'Papal indulgences must
be preached with caution, lest people mistakenly imagine them to
be preferable to other good works of charity.'

The muddy reputation attaching to indulgences has been hard
to shift. There remains a perception that they are a substitute for
actual good deeds, to be used like a Monopoly player uses his 'Get

out of Jail Free' card. In a bid to remedy this problem, in 1967,
Pope Paul VI promulgated his *Indulgentiarum Doctrina*, an apostolic
constitution which sought to redefine and clarify a concept and
practice which, in the pontiff's opinion, 'have a solid foundation
in divine revelation'.

To understand the concept properly and to feel its efficacy, one
must believe in sin and in the will and power of God to confer retribution or forgiveness. One must also be certain that wrongdoings
in this life are to be atoned for here on earth, and that those sins
for which one has not atoned will be dealt with in purgatory after
death, burned away by purifying fire, so that one's damaged soul
may be cleansed and healed and made ready for Heaven.

The Enchiridion of Indulgences, a handbook issued by the Sacred
Apostolic Penitentiary (available online in pdf format), defines an
indulgence as:

> The remission before God of the temporal punishment due
> for sins already forgiven as far as their guilt is concerned. This
> remission the faithful with the proper dispositions and under
> certain determined conditions acquire through the interven-
> tion of the Church.

The Church, in other words, drawing on the so-called Treasury of
Merit, a sort of fund of grace built up by the virtue of Christ, the
Virgin and all the saints, can confer on confessed, repentant and
forgiven sinners, a cancellation of the penalties they must pay on
earth for the wrongdoings they have committed. The definition of
a few terms might help:

Temporal punishment: There are two types of punishment for
sin: eternal and temporal. Eternal punishment means going to

Hell. Temporal punishments are the afflictions suffered here on earth. If you do not either suffer or gain remission from all due temporal punishment before you die, you will have to undergo the purification of your soul in Purgatory after death.

Forgiven sin: God is just: He demands punishment for sin. He is also merciful: He forgives those who truly repent. Forgiveness is obtained by the mediation of the Sacrament of Penance, that is, confession.

Proper dispositions: To gain an indulgence one must be properly disposed to do so. This involves being sincerely repentant—although as Luther pertinently points out: 'No one is sure of the integrity of his own contrition.' Nevertheless, one must make an effort. 'Repent' is one of the watchwords of St Peter, often repeated by him: 'Repent and be baptised for the remission of sins' (*Acts 2:38*); 'Repent ye that your sins may be blotted out' (*Acts 3:19*). One must also be genuinely desirous of obtaining the indulgence and must rid oneself of all attachment to sin, even venial sin.

Determined conditions: To gain an indulgence, one must be in a state of grace. One must be baptised, one must confess the sin, obtain forgiveness for it, take Holy Communion and pray for the intention of the Holy Father, with a *Hail Mary* and an *Our Father*.

Once these preconditions have been fulfilled, an indulgence may be obtained by the performance of certain determined works. Indulgences are either plenary or partial. This means that they either remove all of the temporal penalty for sin, or a part of it. Three general grants are mentioned, in other words, there are three general types of pious behaviour that one may adopt in order to obtain partial indulgence. These are: raising one's mind to God; giving of oneself or of one's goods; voluntarily foregoing legitimate pleasures. This is important, as the main point of all of this is not to clock up indulgences but to become a better person, habitually. On the subject of general grants, no one says it better than St Peter himself: 'Above all things have fervent charity among yourselves: for charity shall cover the multitude of sins...[and] think it not strange concerning the fiery trial which is to try you: but rejoice, inasmuch as ye are partakers of Christ's sufferings.' (*1 Peter 4*).

Plenary indulgences, in Rome, with the above conditions being fulfilled, are granted for performance of the following (NB: only one plenary indulgence can be granted in a single day):

- A visit to one of the four papal basilicas (*see p. 55*) and the reciting there of an *Our Father* and the Creed;
- Receiving the blessing of the pope (*see p. 84*);
- A visit to one of the catacombs (*see p. 105*);
- A visit to one of the Stational Churches during Lent (*see opposite*) and participating in divine service there;
- Performing the exercise of the Way of the Cross, moving between the fourteen Stations of the Cross and meditating before each one (for example on the approach to the Chapel of the Relics in Santa Croce in Gerusalemme; *see p. 94*);
- Ascending the Scala Santa (*see p. 68*).

STATIONAL CHURCHES

The tradition of the stational church dates back to the early years of Christianity, when on certain appointed days the community of the faithful would gather in a designated church to hear Mass celebrated by their bishop. The system fundamentally reflects the fact that, as the early Church expanded, bishops could not officiate at every service. Instead they would make their appearance on certain specified occasions. Today the tradition is kept up during the Lenten season. Below is the list of the Roman stational churches appointed for each day of Lent. On certain occasions the pope officiates at the Mass (to find out at which services the pope will officiate, check the Vatican website, www.vatican.va and click on 'Liturgical Celebrations'). The churches in the list below are some of the oldest and most venerable foundations in the city. Churches in bold type are described in more detail elsewhere in this book. Page references are given. For those with no description, a map reference is provided.

Ash Wednesday and the days following

Ash Wednesday	**S. Sabina** (*p. 116*)
Thursday	S. Giorgio in Velabro (*map p. 302, C3*)
Friday	**SS. Giovanni e Paolo** (*p. 127*)
Saturday	**S. Agostino** (*p. 164*)
First Sunday in Lent	**St John Lateran** (*p. 56*)

Week One

Monday	**S. Pietro in Vincoli** (*p. 21*)
Tuesday	S. Anastasia (*map p. 302, C4*)
Wednesday	**S. Maria Maggiore** (*p. 86*)

Thursday	**S. Lorenzo in Panisperna** (*p. 159*)
Friday	**SS. Apostoli** (*p. 166*)
Saturday	**St Peter's** (*p. 70*)
Second Sunday in Lent	**S. Maria in Domnica** (*p. 129*)

Week Two

Monday	**S. Clemente** (*p. 138*)
Tuesday	**S. Balbina** (*p. 124*)
Wednesday	**S. Cecilia** (*p. 144*)
Thursday	**S. Maria in Trastevere** (*p. 142*)
Friday	S. Vitale (*map p. 303, D2*)
Saturday	SS. Marcellino e Pietro (*map p. 303, F4*)
Third Sunday in Lent	**S. Lorenzo fuori le Mura** (*p. 98*)

Week Three

Monday	S. Marco (*map p. 302, C2*)
Tuesday	**S. Pudenziana** (*p. 16*)
Wednesday	**S. Sisto Vecchio** (*p. 24*)
Thursday	**SS. Cosma e Damiano** (*p. 173*)
Friday	**S. Lorenzo in Lucina** (*p. 184*)
Saturday	**S. Susanna** (*p. 195*)
Fourth Sunday in Lent	**S. Croce in Gerusalemme** (*p. 93*)

Week Four

Monday	**SS. Quattro Coronati** (*p. 134*)
Tuesday	**S. Lorenzo in Damaso** (*p. 182*)
Wednesday	**S. Paolo fuori le Mura** (*p. 45*)
Thursday	SS. Silvestro e Martino (*map p. 303, E3*)
Friday	S. Eusebio (*map p. 303, F2*)
Saturday	**S. Nicola in Carcere** (*p. 218*)
Fifth Sunday in Lent	**St Peter's** (*p. 70*)

Week Five

Monday	**S. Crisogono** (*p. 141*)
Tuesday	**S. Maria in via Lata** (*pp. 39–40*)
Wednesday	S. Marcello (*map p. 302, C2*)
Thursday	S. Apollinare (*map p. 302, B1*)
Friday	**S. Stefano Rotondo** (*p. 131*)
Saturday	S. Giovanni a Porta Latina (*map p. 301, D2*)

Holy Week

Palm Sunday	**St John Lateran** (*p. 56*)
Monday	**S. Prassede** (*p. 191*)
Tuesday	**S. Prisca** (*p. 123*)
Wednesday	**S. Maria Maggiore** (*p. 86*)
Thursday	**St John Lateran** (*p. 56*)
Friday	**S. Croce in Gerusalemme** (*p. 93*)
Saturday	**St John Lateran** (*p. 56*)
Easter Sunday	**S. Maria Maggiore** (*p. 86*)

Octave of Easter

Monday	**St Peter's** (*p. 70*)
Tuesday	**S. Paolo fuori le Mura** (*p. 45*)
Wednesday	**S. Lorenzo fuori le Mura** (*p. 98*)
Thursday	**SS. Apostoli** (*p. 166*)
Friday	**Pantheon** (*p. 217*)
Saturday	**St John Lateran** (*p. 56*)
First Sunday after Easter	**S. Pancrazio** (*p. 189*)

FEAST DAYS

Below is a list of feast days of saints and blesseds whose churches, dedicated altars or burial places—which one might visit on the appropriate day—are featured in this book. In many cases it is clear which church will be relevant. On the feast day of Santa Prisca, the church to seek out is Santa Prisca ('S. Prisca' in the index). In cases where it is not immediately obvious which church is applicable, the answer is supplied in brackets:

January

3rd	Most Holy Name of Jesus (Gesù)
18th	Prisca
20th	Sebastian
21st	Agnes
22nd	Vincent and Anastasius (SS. Vincenzo e Anastasio)
25th	Conversion of St Paul (celebrated at San Paolo fuori le Mura)
31st	Bl. Ludovica Albertoni (S. Francesco a Ripa)

February

7th	Bl. Pius IX (S. Lorenzo fuori le Mura)
14th	Valentine
22nd	Chair of St Peter (Papal Mass in St Peter's)

March

19th	Joseph (S. Giuseppe dei Falegnami)

31st   Balbina

April

29th   Catherine of Siena (S. Maria sopra Minerva)
30th   Pius V (S. Maria Maggiore)

May

3rd   Philip and James (SS. Apostoli)
12th   Pancras (S. Pancrazio);
           Nereus and Achilleus (SS. Nereo e Achilleo)
14th   Matthias (S. Maria Maggiore)
19th   Formerly the feast of Praxedes (Prassede) and
           Pudentiana
26th   Philip Neri (Chiesa Nuova)

June

5th   Boniface (S. Alessio)
9th   Primus and Felicianus (S. Stefano Rotondo)
24th   Birth of St John the Baptist (celebrated in and around
           the basilica of St John Lateran)
26th   Giovanni e Paolo
29th   Peter (St Peter's, S. Pietro in Vincoli);
           Paul (S. Paolo fuori le Mura, S. Paolo alla Regola,
           S. Paolo alle Tre Fontane)

July

17th   Alexis (S. Alessio)

31st   Ignatius Loyola (Gesù)

August

1st   Alfonso
5th   Santa Maria Maggiore (miracle of the snowfall)
7th   Sixtus II (S. Sisto)
10th   Lawrence (S. Lorenzo fuori le Mura, S. Lorenzo in
               Lucina, S. Lorenzo in Damaso, S. Lorenzo in
               Panisperna);
11th   Susanna
12th   Bl. Innocent XI (St Peter's)
18th   Helen, mother of Constantine (S. Maria in Aracoeli,
               S. Croce in Gerusalemme)
24th   Bartholomew (S. Bartolomeo)
27th   Monica (S. Agostino, S. Aurea)
28th   Augustine of Hippo (S. Agostino)
29th   Martyrdom of St John the Baptist (St John Lateran,
               S. Silvestro in Capite);
               Sabina

September

3rd   Gregory the Great (S. Gregorio Magno)
14th   Exaltation of the Holy Cross (S. Croce in Gerusalemme)
26th   Cosmas and Damian (SS. Cosma e Damiano)

October

4th   Francis (S. Francesco a Ripa)
14th   Calixtus (S. Callisto)

22nd	Bl. John Paul II (St Peter's)
28th	Simon and Jude (St Peter's)

November

8th	Four Crowned Saints (SS. Quattro Coronati)
9th	Dedication of St John Lateran
22nd	Cecilia
23rd	Clement
24th	Chrysogonus (S. Crisogono)

December

3rd	Francis Xavier (Gesù)
6th	Nicholas (S. Nicola in Carcere)
26th	Stephen (S. Stefano Rotondo)
27th	John the Evangelist (St John Lateran)
31st	Sylvester (S. Silvestro in Capite, SS. Quattro Coronati)

PRAYERS

Morning Prayer (Collect for Grace)

O Lord our heavenly Father, Almighty and everlasting God, who hast safely brought us to the beginning of this day, defend us in the same with thy mighty power; and grant that this day we fall into no sin, neither run into any kind of danger; but that all our doings may be ordered by thy governance, to do always what is righteous in thy sight; through Jesus Christ our Lord. Amen.

The Nicene Creed

I believe in one God, the Father Almighty,
Maker of heaven and earth,
And of all things visible and invisible;
And in one Lord Jesus Christ,
The only begotten Son of God,
Begotten of his Father before all worlds,
God of God, Light of Light,
Very God of very God,
Begotten, not made,
Being of one substance with the Father;
By whom all things were made;
Who for us men and for our salvation came down from heaven,
And was incarnate by the Holy Ghost of the Virgin Mary,
And was made man;
And was crucified also for us under Pontius Pilate;
He suffered and was buried;
And the third day he rose again according to the Scriptures,
And ascended into heaven,
And sitteth on the right hand of the Father;

And he shall come again with glory, *
To judge both the quick and the dead;
Whose kingdom shall have no end.
I believe in the Holy Ghost the Lord, and Giver of Life,
Who proceedeth from the Father and the Son;
Who with the Father and the Son together is worshipped and
    glorified;
Who spake by the Prophets.
And I believe one holy Catholic and Apostolic Church;
I acknowledge one baptism for the remission of sins;
And I look for the resurrection of the dead,
And the life of the world to come. Amen.

The Apostles' Creed

I believe in God the Father Almighty,
Maker of heaven and earth:
And in Jesus Christ his only Son our Lord,
Who was conceived by the Holy Ghost,
Born of the Virgin Mary,
Suffered under Pontius Pilate,
Was crucified, dead, and buried,
He descended into hell;
The third day he rose again from the dead,
He ascended into heaven,
And sitteth on the right hand of God the Father Almighty;
From thence he shall come to judge the quick and the dead.
I believe in the Holy Ghost;
The holy Catholic Church;
The communion of saints;
The forgiveness of sins;
The resurrection of the body;
And the life everlasting. Amen.

The *Gloria in Excelsis* or Greater Doxology

Glory be to God on high, and in earth peace, goodwill towards men.

We praise thee, we bless thee, we worship thee, we glorify thee, we give thanks to thee for thy great glory.

O Lord God, heavenly King, God the Father Almighty.

O Lord, the only-begotten Son, Jesus Christ; O Lord God, Lamb of God, Son of the Father, that takest away the sins of the world, have mercy upon us, thou that takest away the sins of the world, receive our prayer. Thou that sittest at the right hand of God the Father, have mercy upon us.

For thou only art holy; thou only art the Lord; thou only, O Christ, with the Holy Ghost, art most high in the glory of God the Father. Amen.

The *Gloria Patri* or Lesser Doxology

Glory be to the Father and to the Son and to the Holy Ghost.
As it was in the beginning, is now and ever shall be,
World without end. Amen.

The Hail Mary (*Ave Maria*)

Ave Maria, gratia plena,
Dominus tecum,
Benedicta tu in mulieribus, et benedictus fructus ventris tui Jesus.
Sancta Maria mater Dei,
Ora pro nobis peccatoribus, nunc, et in hora mortis nostrae. Amen.

Hail Mary, full of grace, the Lord is with thee, blessed art thou among women, and blessed is the fruit of thy womb, Jesus. Holy Mary, mother of God, pray for us sinners, now, and in the hour of our death. Amen.

The Our Father (*Pater Noster*)

Our Father, which art in Heaven
Hallowed be thy name
Thy Kingdom come
Thy will be done in earth as it is in Heaven
Give us this day our daily bread
And forgive us our trespasses
As we forgive them that trespass against us
And lead us not into temptation
But deliver us from evil
For thine is the kingdom, the power and the glory
For ever and ever. Amen.

A short grace before meals

Benedictus benedicat. Per Jesum Christum Dominum Nostrum. Amen.

He is blessed. May he bless [what we are about to receive]. Through Jesus Christ Our Lord. Amen.

A short grace after meals

Benedicto benedicatur. Per Jesum Christum Dominum Nostrum. Amen.

Let praise be given to him who is blessed. Through Jesus Christ Our Lord. Amen.

Evening Prayer (Collect for Aid against all Perils)

Lighten our darkness, we beseech thee, O Lord; and by thy great mercy defend us from all perils and dangers of this night; for the love of thy only Son, our Saviour, Jesus Christ. Amen.

GLOSSARY

Adventus, in ancient Roman days, the ceremonial entry of an emperor into a city

Agnus Dei, Latin for 'Lamb of God', in other words, Christ

Annunciation, the appearance of the Archangel Gabriel to Mary with the news that she is to give birth to a son; in art, the depiction of this scene

Amphora (pl. amphorae), large two-handled jar for oil or other liquids

Apostate, someone who commits apostasy, who formally renounces their religion

Architrave, horizontal beam or slab, for example topping a colonnade; the lintel running above the columns of a Classical temple porch

Arian, a follower of Arius, a fourth-century Christian declared heretical for his belief that the divinity of Christ was not equivalent to the divinity of the Father

Assumption, the ascension of the Virgin to heaven, 'assumed' by the power of God

Attribute, symbol or token by which a depicted saint may be recognised. St Peter's attributes are the keys of Heaven; St Jerome's are a lion or cardinal's hat; St Clement's is an anchor. A martyr's attribute, beside the palm frond of victory, is often the instrument by which he or she was done to death, hence the gridiron for St Lawrence

Basilica, see p. 54

Chi Rho, Christological symbol formed of the superimposed letters X and P, the first two letters of the word Christ in Greek

Confessio, crypt beneath the high altar of a church, containing precious relics

Cosmatesque, a technique of decorative stone inlay, its name derived from two craftsmen called Cosma, who used fragments of ancient marbles, chiefly purple and green, to create inlaid geometric patterns on floors and other surfaces

Composite, a column capital which combines the Corinthian acanthus leaf with the Ionic volute or scroll

Corinthian, the name given to an order of Classical architecture distinguished by its tall, slender fluted columns and capitals decorated with curling acanthus leaves

Counter-Reformation, Roman Catholic movement originating in the sixteenth century in response to the rise of Protestantism; a bid to prevent the defection of congregations to the reform movements. It gave rise not only to the infamous Inquisition but also to substantial reforms within the Roman Catholic church

Curia, the papal 'court'; the administrative body of the Holy See

Deacon, literally, a servant or messenger of the Church, in early times often associated with charitable work

Evangelists, Matthew, Mark, Luke and John, the authors of the four gospels, often represented in art by their symbols: man (Matthew), lion (Mark), bull (Luke) and eagle (John)

Gammadion (pl. gammadia), see p. 175

Holy Year, see p. 74

Labarum, military standard consisting of a flag suspended from a cross; it was adopted by the armies of Constantine

Mithras, see p. 140

Pallium (pl. pallia), an ecclesiastical stole (*see p. 154*)

Parian, a fine white marble from the island of Paros, Greece

Passion, the sufferings of Christ in the days leading up to and including his crucifixion and death

Porphyry, a dark blue or purple stone much prized in the ancient world and used almost exclusively for imperial commissions

Sibyl, in the ancient world, a prophetess

Solomonic, twisted or 'barley-sugar' column, so called because the columns of the Temple of Solomon are supposed to have been of this type

Spolia, architectural elements removed from one building and reused in another; many Roman churches, for example, have columns which are spolia from earlier temples

Strigilated, decorated with a pattern of undulating parallel grooves, shallowly carved

Titulus (pl. tituli), see p. 122

Translation, of relics, their removal from one location to another, usually of greater prominence

Travertine, whitish-beige limestone containing darker striations, quarried at Tivoli and much used in the buildings of Rome

Triptych, a panel painting in three 'leaves' or sections

Triumphal arch, in a basilica, the archway marking the division between nave and apse

Trompe l'oeil, literally 'fooling the eye', a term used to describe illusionist art, where a sense of three-dimensionality is created on a two-dimensional surface

KEY DATES IN ROMAN HISTORY

753 BC: Romulus founds Rome, according to legend. The first settlement is on the Palatine Hill;

509 BC: Tarquinius Superbus, last king of Rome, is ousted and the Republic is established;

246–146 BC: The Punic Wars are fought by Rome against the Carthaginians. Rome emerges victorious, gaining control of Sicily, parts of Spain and north Africa;

44 BC: Amid fears that he intends to disband the Republic and institute a monarchy, Julius Caesar is murdered near the present-day Largo Torre Argentina (*map p. 302, B2*) and is cremated in the Forum;

31 BC: Octavian (later Augustus), Caesar's adopted son, ends the struggle for power when he triumphs over the forces of Mark Antony and Cleopatra. Rome gains control of Egypt;

AD 49: According to Suetonius, Jews are expelled from Rome by the emperor Claudius, perhaps because of dissent among them caused by conversions to Christianity;

AD 64: Somewhere around this date, St Peter is martyred under Nero, and buried on the site of the present St Peter's Basilica;

AD 65: At about this time, St Paul is martyred under Nero, and buried on the site of the present San Paolo fuori le Mura;

AD 96–180: The era of the 'Five Good Emperors': Nerva, Trajan, Hadrian, Antoninus Pius and Marcus Aurelius. It is during the reign of Trajan that the Roman Empire reaches its greatest extent;

125: The Pantheon is constructed by Hadrian;

258: Murder of Pope Sixtus II and martyrdom of St Lawrence, during the persecutions of Valerian. The bodies of Sts Peter and Paul may have been moved to the catacombs for temporary safekeeping;

303: Beginning of the persecutions of Diocletian. Pope Marcellinus is ordered to sacrifice to the gods, and may have done so. Two traditions exist, one of his apostasy, the other declaring him to have died a martyr's death;

312: Constantine defeats the rival emperor Maxentius at the Milvian Bridge, north of Rome's city centre;

313: Constantine's Edict of Tolerance gives freedom of worship to Christians. Soon after this, Constantine gives a grant of land to Pope Miltiades for the building of a permanent church. The resulting basilica of St John Lateran is Rome's first officially sanctioned Christian place of worship;

330: Death of Helen, mother of Constantine. She is buried in a mausoleum in Rome; Constantine dedicates the city of New Rome (Constantinople), transferring his capital there;

337: Baptism and death of Constantine;

378–81: Emperor Theodosius I declares Nicene Christianity the state religion. He has a staunch supporter in Rome in the form of Pope Damasus;

387: St Augustine in Rome. His mother Monica dies at Ostia;

410: Rome sacked by the Goths; St Augustine writes his *City of God* to address fears that the sack was the retribution of the pagan gods, taking revenge for their ousting;

476: The last Emperor of the West, Romulus Augustulus, abdicates and Rome is taken over by the Goths;

483: Death of Pope Simplicius, under whom the first of Rome's pagan buildings had been converted into a church;

549: Games are held in the Circus Maximus for the last time;

609: Consecration of the Pantheon, the first pagan temple to become a church;

625–38: Pontificate of Honorius I, a great embellisher of churches in Rome built over martyrs' graves;

754–56: The Frankish king Pepin takes Ravenna from the Lombards and presents it to the pope. The temporal rule of the papacy begins;

800: Charlemagne, King of the Franks, is crowned Emperor of the Romans in St Peter's by Pope Leo III;

817–24: Pontificate of Paschal I, an unpopular pope but one who left a great legacy in the form of beautiful church mosaics;

1084: Rome sacked by the Normans under Robert Guiscard;

1204: Soldiers on the Fourth Crusade, preached by Pope Innocent III to retake Jerusalem from the Muslims, make a detour to Constantinople, sack it and capture it for the Latin Church. The pope is horrified, although many precious relics find their way to Rome as a result;

1209: St Francis comes to Rome to seek permission to found an order from Pope Honorius III;

1216–17: St Dominic receives permission from Pope Honorius III to lead an order of preaching friars;

1300: Boniface VIII proclaims the first Holy Year. A record number of pilgrims comes to Rome;

1309: Pope Clement V moves his seat to Avignon under pressure from the French king. As the Catholic Church splits, the competing series of papal pretenders in Rome are known as 'antipopes';

1377: The Holy See returns to Rome under Gregory XI. The popes take up residence in the Vatican;

1417: Martin V ends the years of schism between popes and antipopes;

1503–13: Julius II founds the Swiss Guard, and commissions Michelangelo to paint the Sistine Chapel ceiling;

1511: Martin Luther visits Rome and is critical of the papacy;

1527: Rome is sacked by the troops of the Holy Roman Emperor Charles V during struggles for power between pope and emperor. Pope Clement VII takes refuge in Castel Sant'Angelo;

1555: The Counter-Reformation gets into its stride with the election of Pope Paul IV. Suspecting the Jews of Rome to be in league with the Protestants, he confines them to a ghetto;

1556: St Ignatius Loyola dies in Rome;

1626: The new St Peter's Basilica is consecrated by Pope Urban VIII;

1797: Napoleon Bonaparte leads the French armies into Rome;

1808–09: Napoleon occupies Rome and imprisons Pope Pius VII;

1849: The Republic of Italy is established by Mazzini and Garibaldi in Rome. French troops regain control of the city later that same year. Much damage is done during the fighting. The relics of St Pancras (San Pancrazio) are desecrated;

1870: Rome falls to Italian troops. Pope Pius IX refuses to recognise the regime, is relieved of temporal power and is confined to the Vatican;

1871: Rome becomes the capital of Italy;

1914–19: First World War. Pope Benedict XV's pleas for a truce are ignored; Italy enters the war on the Allied side; the Vatican is excluded from the Peace Conference in 1919;

1922: Mussolini marches on Rome and seizes power;

1929: The Lateran Pact is signed between Mussolini and Pius XI, defining the relationship between Church and state;

1943–44: German occupation of Rome, but not the Vatican City, which had remained neutral; Rome's Jews are deported; the Allies enter Rome in 1944;

1978: The Polish cardinal Karol Wojtyla is elected pope, the first non-Italian pontiff since 1523. He takes the regnal name John Paul II;

2005: Election of Cardinal Joseph Ratzinger as pope. He takes the name Benedict XVI;

2011: Beatification of John Paul II. He is reinterred in St Peter's Basilica.

KINGS & EMPERORS

Kings of Rome

Romulus	753–716 BC
Numa Pompilius	716–673 BC
Tullus Hostilius	673–640 BC
Ancus Martius	640–616 BC
Tarquinius Priscus	616–579 BC
Servius Tullius	579–534 BC
Tarquinius Superbus	534–509 BC

Roman Republic

Sulla (dictator)	82–78 BC
First Triumvirate (Julius Caesar, Crassus, Pompey)	60–53 BC
Pompey (dictator)	52–47 BC
Julius Caesar (dictator)	45–44 BC
Second Triumvirate (Mark Antony, Lepidus, Octavian)	43–27 BC

Roman Empire

Augustus (formerly Octavian)	27 BC–AD 14
Tiberius	14–37
Caligula	37–41
Claudius	41–54
Nero	54–68
Galba	68–69
Otho	69
Vitellius	69
Vespasian	69–79
Titus	79–81
Domitian	81–96
Nerva	96–98
Trajan	98–117
Hadrian	117–138
Antoninus Pius	138–161
Marcus Aurelius	161–180
Lucius Verus (co-emperor)	161–169
Commodus	180–192
Pertinax	193
Didius Julianus	193
Septimius Severus	193–211
Caracalla	211–217
Geta (co-emperor)	211–212
Macrinus	217–218
Elagabalus	218–222
Alexander Severus	222–235
Maximinus Thrax	235–238
Gordian I	238
Gordian II	238
Pupienus	238
Balbinus (co-emperor)	238
Gordian III	238–244
Philip I	244–247
Philip II	247–249
Decius	249–251
Gallus and Volusian	251–253
Aemilianus	253
Valerian	253–260
Gallienus	260–268
Claudius II	268–270
Quintillus	270
Aurelian	270–275
Domitianus II (usurper)	270–271
Tacitus	275–276
Florian	276
Probus	276–282
Carus	282–283
Carinus	282–285

Numerian (co-emperor)	283–284
Diocletian (institutes tetrarchy)	285–305
Maximian (co-emperor)	286–305
Constantius Chlorus	305–306
Galerius	305–310
Licinius	308–324
Flavius Severus	306–307
Maxentius	306–312

Christian Empire

Constantine the Great (baptised 337)	306–337
Constantine II	337–340
Constans (co-emperor)	337–350
Constantius II (co-emperor)	337–361
Magnentius (co-emperor)	350–353
Julian the Apostate (reverts to pagansim)	361–363
Jovian	363–364
Valentinian I (in West)	364–375
Valens (in East)	364–378
Gratian	367–383
Valentinian II (usurper)	375–392
Theodosius I	378–395

Empire of the West

Honorius	395–423
Valentinian III	425–55
Petronius Maximus	455
Avitus	455–456
Majorian	457–461
Libius Severus	461–465
Anthemius	467–472
Olybrius	472

Glycerius	473
Julius Nepos	474–475
Romulus Augustulus	475–476

Goths, Byzantines, Lombards

Control of the Western Empire is contested between these powers from the late fifth to the mid-eighth century.

Temporal rule of the Popes

Traditionally dated from the years 754–56, when Pepin, father of Charlemagne, wrests Ravenna from the Byzantines and presents it to Pope Stephen III. Though frequently challenged by other rulers (Holy Roman Emperors, Napoleon), the popes continue to hold power in their so-called Papal States until 1870. For the names and dates of all the popes, see next section.

Kings of Italy

Vittorio Emanuele II (ruled in Rome from 1870)	1861–78
Umberto I	1878–1900
Vittorio Emanuele III	1900–46
Umberto II	1946

THE SUPREME PONTIFFS

Dates for some of the early martyred popes are conjectural. The names of papal rivals or otherwise disputed claimants to the pontifical throne are given in square brackets.

1. **St Peter**, martyr; 42–67
2. **St Linus**, martyr; 67–78
3. **St Anacletus I**, martyr; 78–90
4. **St Clement I**, martyr; 90–99
5. **St Evaristus**, martyr; 99–105
6. **St Alexander I**; 105–115
7. **St Sixtus I**, martyr; 115–125
8. **St Telesphorus**, martyr; 125–?136
9. **St Hyginus**, martyr; 136–140
10. **St Pius I**, martyr; 140–155
11. **St Anicetus**, martyr; 155–166
12. **St Soter**, martyr; 166–175
13. **St Eleutherius**, martyr; 175–189
14. **St Victor I**, martyr; 189–199
15. **St Zephyrinus**, martyr; 199–217
16. **St Calixtus**, martyr; 217–222
    [**St Hippolytus**, 217–235]
17. **St Urban I**, martyr; 222–230
18. **St Pontianus**, martyr; 230–235
19. **St Anterus**, martyr; 235–236
20. **St Fabian**, martyr; 236–250
21. **St Cornelius**, martyr; 251–253
    [**Novatian**, 251–258]

22. **St Lucius I**, martyr; 253–254
23. **St Stephen I**, martyr; 254–257
24. **St Sixtus II**, martyr; 257–258
25. **St Dionysius**, martyr; 259–268
26. **St Felix I**, martyr; 269–274
27. **St Eutychianus**, martyr; 275–283
28. **St Gaius**, martyr; 283–296
29. **St Marcellinus**, ?martyr; 296–304
30. **St Marcellus I**, martyr; 308–309
31. **St Eusebius**, martyr; 309–?310
32. **St Miltiades**, martyr; 311–314
33. **St Sylvester I**, 314–335
34. **St Mark**, 336
35. **St Julius I**, 337–352
36. **Liberius**, 352–366
    [**St Felix II**, 355–365]
37. **St Damasus I**, 366–384
    [**Ursinus**, 366–367]
38. **St Siricius**, 384–399
39. **St Anastasius I**, 399–401
40. **St Innocent I**, 401–417

41. **St Zosimus**, 417–18
    [**Eulalius** 418–19]
42. **St Boniface I**, 418–422
43. **St Celestine I**, 422–432
44. **St Sixtus III**, 432–440
45. **St Leo I, the Great**, 440–461
46. **St Hilarius**, 461–468
47. **St Simplicius**, 468–483
48. **St Felix III** (II), 483–492
49. **St Gelasius I**, 492–496
50. **St Anastasius II**, 496–498
51. **St Symmachus**, 498–514
    [**Laurentius**, 498–505]
52. **St Hormisdas**, 514–523
53. **St John I**, martyr; 523–526
54. **St Felix IV (III)**, 526–530
55. **Boniface II**, 530–532
    [**Dioscurus**, 530]
56. **John II**, 533–535
57. **St Agapitus I**, 535–536
58. **St Silverius**, martyr; 536–537
59. **Vigilius**, 538–555
60. **Pelagius I**, 556–561
61. **John III**, 561–574
62.**Benedict I**, 575–579
63. **Pelagius II**, 579–590
64. **St Gregory I, the Great**, 590–604
65. **Sabinianus**, 604–606
66. **Boniface III**, 607
67. **St Boniface IV**, 608–615
68. **St Adeodatus I**, 615–618
69. **Boniface V**, 619–625
70. **Honorius I**, 625–638
71. **Severinus**, 640
72. **John IV**, 640–642
73. **Theodore I**, 642–649

74. **St Martin I**, martyr; 649–655
75. **St Eugenius I**, 655–657
76. **St Vitalian**, 657–672
77. **Adeodatus II**, 672–676
78. **Donus**, 676–678
79. **St Agatho**, 678–681
80. **St Leo II**, 682–683
81. **St Benedict II**, 684–685
82. **John V**, 685–686
83. **Conon**, 686–687
    [**Theodore**, 687]
    [**Paschal**, 687]
84. **St Sergius I**, 687–701
85. **John VI**, 701–705
86. **John VII**, 705–707
87. **Sisinnius**, 708
88. **Constantine**, 708–715
89. **St Gregory II**, 715–731
90. **St Gregory III**, 731–741
91. **St Zacharias**, 741–752
92. **Stephen II**, 752
93. **Stephen III**, 752–757
94. **St Paul I**, 757– 767
    [**Constantine II**, 767–769]
    [**Philip**, 768]
95. **Stephen IV**, 768–772
96. **Hadrian I**, 772–795
97. **St Leo III**, 795–816
98. **St Stephen V**, 816–817
99. **St Paschal I**, 817–824
100. **Eugenius II**, 824–827
101. **Valentine**, 827
102. **Gregory IV**, 827–844
103. **Sergius II**, 844–847
    [**John**, 844]
104. **St Leo IV**, 847–855
105. **Benedict III**, 855–858
    [**Anastasius**, 855]

106. **St Nicholas, I the Great,** 858–867
107. **Hadrian II,** 867–872
108 **John VIII,** 872–882
109. **Marinus I** (Martin II) 882–884
110. **St Hadrian III,** 884–885
111. **Stephen VI,** 885–891
112. **Formosus,** 891–896
113. **Boniface VI,** 896
114. **Stephen VII,** 896–897
115. **Romanus,** 897
116. **Theodore II,** 897
117. **John IX,** 898–900
118. **Benedict IV,** 900–903
119. **Leo V,** 903
    [**Christopher,** 903–904]
120. **Sergius III,** 904–911
121. **Anastasius III,** 911–913
122. **Lando,** 913–914
123. **John X,** 914–928
124. **Leo VI,** 928
125. **Stephen VIII,** 929–931
126. **John XI,** 931–935
127. **Leo VII,** 936–939
128. **Stephen IX,** 939–942
129. **Marinus II** (Martin III), 942–946
130. **Agapitus II,** 946–955
131. **John XII,** 955–964
132. **Leo VIII,** 963–965
133. **Benedict V,** 964
134. **John XIII,** 965–972
135. **Benedict VI,** 973–974
    [**Boniface VII,** first claim, 974]
136. **Benedict VII,** 974–983
137. **John XIV,** 983–984
    [**Boniface VII,** second claim, 984–985]

138. **John XV,** 985–996
139. **Gregory V,** 996–999
    [**John XVI,** 997–998]
140. **Sylvester II,** 999–1003
141. **John XVII,** 1003
142. **John XVIII,** 1004–09
143. **Sergius IV,** 1009–12
144. **Benedict VIII,** 1012–24
    [**Gregory,** 1012]
145. **John XIX,** 1024–32
146. **Benedict IX,** 1032–45 and 1047–48
147. **Sylvester III,** 1045
148. **Gregory VI,** 1045–46
149. **Clement II,** 1046–47
150. **Damasus II,** 1048
151. **St Leo IX,** 1049–54
152. **Victor II,** 1055–57
153. **Stephen X,** 1057–58
    [**Benedict X,** 1058–59]
154. **Nicholas II,** 1059–61
155. **Alexander II,** 1061–73
    [**Honorius II,** 1061–72]
156. **St Gregory VII,** 1073–85
    [**Clement III,** 1080–1100]
157. **Bl. Victor III,** 1086–87
158. **Bl. Urban II,** 1088–99
159. **Paschal II,** 1099–1118
    [**Theodoric,** 1100]
    [**Albert,** 1102]
    [**Sylvester IV,** 1105–11]
160. **Gelasius II,** 1118–19
    [**Gregory VIII,** 1118–21]
161. **Calixtus II,** 1119–24
    [**Celestine,** 1124–25]
162. **Honorius II,** 1124–30
163. **Innocent II,** 1130–43
    [**Anacletus II,** 1130–38]
    [**Victor IV,** 1138]

164. **Celestine II**, 1143–44
165. **Lucius II**, 1144–45
166. **Bl. Eugenius III**, 1145–53
167. **Anastasius IV**, 1153–54
168. **Hadrian IV**, 1154–59
169. **Alexander III**, 1159–81
    [**Victor IV** (V), 1159–64]
    [**Paschal III**, 1164–68]
    [**Calixtus III**, 1168–78]
    [**Innocent III**, 1179–80]
170. **Lucius III**, 1181–85
171. **Urban III**, 1185–87
172. **Gregory VIII**, 1187
173. **Clement III**, 1187–91
174. **Celestine III**, 1191–98
175. **Innocent III**, 1198–1216
176. **Honorius III**, 1216–27
177. **Gregory IX**, 1227–41
178. **Celestine IV**, 1241
179. **Innocent IV**, 1243–54
180. **Alexander IV**, 1254–61
181. **Urban IV**, 1261–64
182. **Clement IV**, 1265–68
183. **Bl. Gregory X**, 1271–76
184. **Bl. Innocent V**, 1276
185. **Hadrian V**, 1276
186. **John XXI**, 1276–77
187. **Nicholas III**, 1277–80
188. **Martin IV**, 1281–85
189. **Honorius IV**, 1285–87
190. **Nicholas IV**, 1288–92
191. **St Celestine V**, 1294
192. **Boniface VIII**, 1294–1303
193. **Bl. Benedict XI**, 1303–04
194. **Clement V**, 1305–14
195. **John XXII**, 1316–34
    [**Nicholas V**, 1328–30]
196. **Benedict XII**, 1334–42
197. **Clement VI**, 1342–52

198. **Innocent VI**, 1352–62
199. **Bl. Urban V**, 1362–70
200. **Gregory XI**, 1370–78
201. **Urban VI**, 1378–89
    [**Clement VII**, 1378–94]
202. **Boniface IX**, 1389–1404
    [**Benedict XIII**, 1394–1423]
203. **Innocent VII**, 1404–06
204. **Gregory XII**, 1406–15
    [**Alexander V**, 1409–10]
    [**John XXIII**, 1410–15]
205. **Martin V**, 1417–31
    [**Clement VIII**, 1423–29]
    [**Benedict XIV**, 1425–?30]
206. **Eugenius IV**, 1431–47
    [**Felix V**, 1439–49]
207. **Nicholas V**, 1447–55
208. **Calixtus III**, 1455–58
209. **Pius II**, 1458–64
210. **Paul II**, 1464–71
211. **Sixtus IV**, 1471–84
212. **Innocent VIII**, 1484–92
213. **Alexander VI**, 1492–1503
214. **Pius III**, 1503
215. **Julius II**, 1503–13
216. **Leo X**, 1513–21
217. **Hadrian VI**, 1522–23
218. **Clement VII**. 1523–34
219. **Paul III**, 1534–49
220. **Julius III**, 1550–55
221. **Marcellus II**, 1555
222. **Paul IV**, 1555–59
223. **Pius IV**, 1559–65
224. **St Pius V**, 1566–72
225. **Gregory XIII**, 1572–85
226. **Sixtus V**, 1585–90
227. **Urban VII**, 1590
228. **Gregory XIV**, 1590–91
229. **Innocent IX**, 1591

230. **Clement VIII**, 1592–1605
231. **Leo XI**, 1605
232. **Paul V**, 1605–21
233. **Gregory XV**, 1621–23
234. **Urban VIII**, 1623–44
235. **Innocent X**, 1644–55
236. **Alexander VII**, 1655–67
237. **Clement IX**, 1667–69
238. **Clement X**, 1670–76
239. **Bl. Innocent XI**, 1676–89
240. **Alexander VIII**, 1689–91
241. **Innocent XII**, 1691–1700
242. **Clement XI**, 1700–21
243. **Innocent XIII**, 1721–24
244. **Benedict XIII**, 1724–30
245. **Clement XII**, 1730–40
246. **Benedict XIV**, 1740–58
247. **Clement XIII**, 1758–69
248. **Clement XIV**, 1769–74
249. **Pius VI**, 1775–99
250. **Pius VII**, 1800–23
251. **Leo XII**, 1823–29
252. **Pius VIII**, 1829–30
253. **Gregory XVI**, 1831–46
254. **Bl. Pius IX**, 1846–78
255. **Leo XIII**, 1878–1903
256. **St Pius X**, 1903–14
257. **Benedict XV**, 1914–22
258. **Pius XI**, 1922–39
259. **Pius XII**, 1939–58
260. **Bl. John XXIII**, 1958–1963
261. **Paul VI**, 1963–78
262. **John Paul I**, 1978
263. **Bl. John Paul II**, 1978–2005
264. **Benedict XVI**, 2005–

BIBLIOGRAPHY

Augustine of Hippo: *Confessions*, Penguin Classics edition, Tr. R.S. Pine-Coffin

Barraclough, Geoffrey: *The Medieval Papacy*, London 1968

Beck-Friis, Johan: *The Protestant Cemetery in Rome*, Malmö 1956 and Rome 2008

Boardman, Jonathan: *Rome, a Cultural and Literary Companion*, Oxford 2000

Bowersock, Glen W., *Peter and Constantine*, in *St Peter's in the Vatican* (ed. W. Tronzo), Cambridge 2005

Brandenburg, Hugo: *The Basilica of S. Agnese and the Mausoleum of Constantina Augusta*, Regensburg 2006

Buranelli, Duston (Eds): *The Fifteenth-Century Frescoes in the Sistine Chapel*, Vatican City 2003

Carletti, Sandro: *Guide to the Catacombs of Priscilla*, Vatican City 2007

Chamay, Jacques: *Ostia: port de la Rome antique*, Geneva 2001

Chamberlin, Russell: *The Bad Popes*, Sutton 2003

Claridge, Amanda: *Rome* (Oxford Archaeological Guides), Oxford 1998

Coarelli, Filippo: *Rome and Environs: An Archaeological Guide* (Tr. Claus and Harmon), California 2007

Cross, F.L. and Livingstone E.A. (Eds): *The Oxford Dictionary of the Christian Church*

D'Atti Monica and Cinti, Franco: *Guida alla Via Francigena*, Milan 2006

Elvins, Mark: *Catholic Trivia*, London 1992

Farmer, David: *The Oxford Dictionary of Saints*

Ferrari-Bravo, Anna (Ed.): *Roma* (Touring Club Italiano), Milan 2002

Freeman, Charles: *Holy Bones, Holy Dust: How Relics Shaped the History of Medieval Europe*, Yale 2011

Freeman, Charles: *Sites of Antiquity: Fifty Sites that Explain the Classical World*, London 2009

Gabucci, Ada: *Rome* (Dictionaries of Civilization), California 2005

Gallico, Sonia: *Guide to the Excavations of Ostia Antica*, Rome 2000

Giustozzi, Nunzio (Ed.): *Castel Sant'Angelo*, Rome 2003

Gregorovius, Ferdinand: *History of the City of Rome in the Middle Ages*

(Tr. Mrs G.A. Hamilton), London 1909

Hesemann, Michael: *Der erste Papst: archäologen auf der Spur des historischen Petrus*, Munich 2003

Hibbard, Howard: *Bernini*, New York and London 1965

Kelly, J.N.D., *The Oxford Dictionary of Popes*

Lampe, Peter: *Christians at Rome in the First Two Centuries* (Tr. M. Steinhauser), London 2003

Macadam, Alta and Barber, Annabel: *Blue Guide Rome* (10th ed.), London 2010

MacDonald, William L.: *The Pantheon: Design, Meaning and Progeny*, Harvard 1976

Morton, H.V.: *A Traveller in Rome*, London 1957

Nes, Solrunn: *The Mystical Language of Icons*, London 2000

Proja, Msgr G. Battista: *Il Battistero Lateranense*, Rome 1999

Scotti, R.A.: *Basilica: The Splendor and the Scandal: Building St Peter's*, New York 2007

Seibert, Jutta (Ed.): *Lexikon Christlicher Kunst*, Freiburg 2002

Stephenson, Paul: *Constantine: Unconquered Emperor, Christian Victor*, London 2009

Suetonius: *The Twelve Caesars*, Penguin Classics edition, Tr. Robert Graves

Ward-Perkins, Bryan: *The Fall of Rome and the End of Civilization*, Oxford 2005

Watkin, David: *The Roman Forum*, London 2009

Webb, Matilda: *The Churches and Catacombs of Early Christian Rome*, Sussex 2001

Online works consulted include: the *Enchiridion of Indulgences*; *The Catholic Encyclopedia* (newadvent.org); Maria Paola di Biagio's *Simboli Cristologici e Iconografia* (larecherche.it) and medievo.roma.it.

INDEX

Numbers in italics are picture references. References with a 'c.' afterwards denote information contained in a caption. Reference with an 'n.' indicate that the information appears in a footnote.

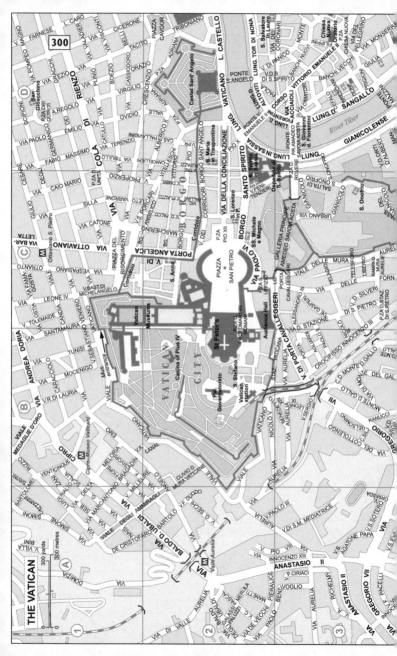

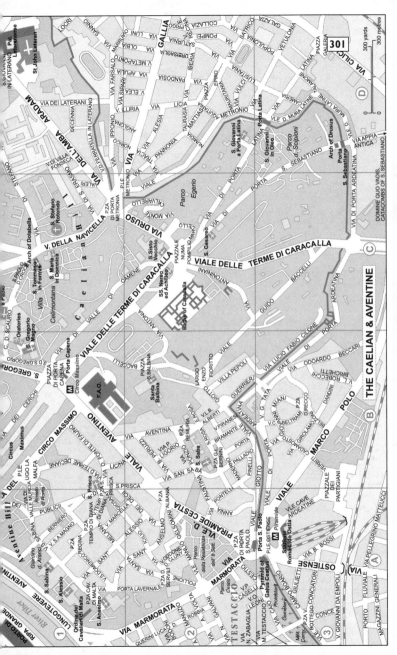

301

THE CAELIAN & AVENTINE

300 yards

300 metres